American Studies

Have you studied out the land, its idioms and men?

Have you learned . . . the politics, geography, pride, freedom, friendship of the land? its substratums and objects?

Have you considered the organic compact of the first day of the first year of Independence, sign'd by the Commissioners, ratified by the States, and read by Washington at the head of the army?

Have you possess'd yourself of the Federal Constitution?

Do you see who have left all feudal processes and poems behind them, and assumed the poems and processes of Democracy?

Are you faithful to things? do you teach what the land and sea, the bodies of men, womanhood, amativeness, heroic angers teach?

Have you fled through fleeting customs, popularities?

Can you hold your hand against all seductions, follies, whirls, fierce contentions? are you strong? are you really of the whole People?

WALT WHITMAN

AMERICAN STUDIES

BY

TREMAINE McDOWELL

1948

THE UNIVERSITY OF MINNESOTA PRESS · MINNEAPOLIS
LONDON · GEOFFREY CUMBERLEGE · OXFORD UNIVERSITY PRESS

PRINTED AT THE NORTH CENTRAL PUBLISHING COMPANY, ST. PAUL

Foreword

ALTHOUGH the immediate subject of this little volume is American Studies, its ultimate concern is with the broad pattern of higher education in the United States. The first two chapters and the last chapter deal with general principles; the intervening chapters are designed to show how those principles actually operate today. Here are discussed, not untested theories, but the aims and achievements of a currently successful program, limited to the American scene for its materials but unlimited in its suggestiveness for the liberalizing of American education. If the author's full purpose is accomplished, this book will encourage the organizing of new programs not only in American Studies but in a variety of other interdisciplinary fields.

American Studies are designed to modify a persistent characteristic of mankind and to advance a contemporary movement in education. The characteristic is the tendency of men to live predominantly in one of the three tenses, past, present, or future, and to forget the other two. This characteristic as it affects higher education is discussed in a chapter entitled "Time and the Colleges." The contemporary movement in education is a trend away from extreme academic specialization toward a synthesis of knowledge. This development is discussed in a chapter entitled "General Education." Against this background and in these terms, American Studies are then described in Chapter III, and the advantages and disadvantages of a curriculum which deals with the student's own way of life are weighed. The curriculums in American civilization which have been organized in the United States (with one exception) and in Europe are presented in the fourth chapter; American courses (both the

v

courses offered by single departments and the new interdepartmental courses) are presented in the fifth. The curriculum, the courses, and the additional activities which
make the Program in American Studies at the University of
Minnesota the most inclusive program now in operation are
described in Chapter VI. Finally, the relationship of American Studies to regional culture, national loyalty, and world
society is examined in Chapter VII.

This book is addressed to all who are concerned with
American civilization or with American education but most
particularly to those who are concerned with both. The discussion, though it deals chiefly with the liberal arts college
and the graduate school, has relevance for the general public
and for high school teachers and administrators. What is
said here has greatest significance, however, for administrators in higher education, for college teachers of the social
sciences and the humanities, and for graduate students and
mature undergraduates who are about to a choose a major
or are already engaged in the study of American culture.

My report on American Studies is based chiefly on first-
hand observation of procedures in more than thirty colleges
and universities (including institutions where programs in
American Studies have been organized and where they have
not). Supplementary information has been derived from cor-
respondence and printed announcements (including data
collected by two committees of which I have been chairman
or member: that on Courses and Curricula in American Civilization appointed by the American Literature Group of the
Modern Language Association and that on American Literature and Civilization appointed by the National Council of
Teachers of English under the chairmanship of Professor
William Crane of the College of the City of New York).

Acknowledgments

I AM grateful to the University of Minnesota for leave of absence and to the Rockefeller Foundation for a grant which made possible much of the travel necessary for the writing of this study. For permission to reprint material from my earlier articles on the topics discussed here, I am obligated to *College English, School and Society,* and *American Heritage.* My warm thanks go to those who (sometimes without accepting all my conclusions) have read and criticized my manuscript: Theodore Hornberger, Henry Nash Smith, Mary C. Turpie, Bernard Bowron, Alice Tyler, Lowry Nelson, and Ralph Nafziger, all associated with the Program in American Studies at the University of Minnesota; Richard Shryock and Robert E. Spiller of the University of Pennsylvania; Norman Holmes Pearson of Yale University; and D. H. Daugherty of the American Council of Learned Societies. I am grateful to the first three friends named above for reading proof when it was impossible for me to do so. My thanks go also to the many people on many campuses who have given me aid and comfort.

T. Mc D.

September 15, 1948

Contents

I

Time and the Colleges

"I ACCEPT Time absolutely," declared Walt Whitman. When Margaret Fuller announced in similar fashion that she accepted the universe, Thomas Carlyle growled: "Gad, she'd better!" We are inclined at first thought to say the same of Whitman. On second thought we recognize that an unqualified acceptance of time — acceptance alike of the past, the present, and the future — may be a notable achievement.

Among three such diverse figures as Henry Ford, Neville Chamberlain, and Oswald Spengler there is little resemblance and yet they have one characteristic in common. Each revealed a capacity for living in a single tense or for questioning the validity of one or both of the other tenses. When Henry Ford testified under oath that he believed history to be bunk, he dramatized his skepticism concerning the past. We are aware that he later recanted and became, if not historically minded, at least antiquarianly inclined. We are also aware that in the same fashion many Americans ignore or minimize the past and that in the university world the same nearsightedness frequently overtakes social scientists.

When Neville Chamberlain persuaded himself that it was possible to live with Hitler on the terms on which Chamberlain in the past had conducted his own personal business in prewar Birmingham, he achieved one of the most monumental denials of the present that this century has witnessed. Other politicians, not only abroad but in the United States (American political parties, remarks a Swedish observer, "in

1

many respects are still living in the nineteenth century"), have shown themselves equally unconscious of the passing of time. So have many teachers of the humanities.

Oswald Spengler in *The Decline of the West* had little hope for the future: "The nineteenth and twentieth centuries, hitherto looked on as the highest point of an ascending line of world-history, are in reality a stage of life which may be observed in every culture that has ripened to its limit." Our fate is to be "used up"; that is to say, "The expansive tendency is a doom . . . which grips, forces into service, and uses up the late mankind of the world-city stage" — meaning us. Such doubt concerning the future develops out of rejection of the present — a rejection exemplified by the critics who in every era deny that their own age can produce great literature, distinguished art, or memorable ideas.

Since acceptance of all three tenses is a major doctrine in American Studies, Whitman's position deserves further examination. Looking into *Leaves of Grass,* we find that his conception of time is an integral part of his democratic faith. He reconciles past, present, and future not by erroneously making them identical, in the manner of certain of the ancients and certain of the neoclassicists, but by stressing their similarity and, most of all, their continuity in an open universe.

> A vast similitude interlocks all . . .
> All lives and death, all of the past, present, and
> future,
> And shall forever span them and compactly hold
> them and enclose them.

This progression of time he interprets in the terms of an interlocking sequence. Speaking not merely for himself but for the present, he announces: "I am an acme of things accomplish'd, and I am an encloser of things to come."

The past commands Whitman's utmost respect:

Dead poets, philosophs, priests,
Martyrs, artists, inventors, governments long since,
Language-shapers on other shores,
Nations once powerful, now reduced, withdrawn, or
    desolate,
I dare not proceed till I respectfully credit what you
    have left, wafted hither.

But for the living, the immediate significance of the past lies in its contribution to our central link. Again speaking for all mankind, he announced:

[I come]
With antecedents,
With my fathers and mothers and the accumulations
    of past ages,
With all which, had it not been, I would not now be
    here, as I am.

Out of the past pours the motive force of the present: "The past is the push of you, me, all," and again:

As a projectile form'd, impell'd, passing a certain
    line, keeps on,
So the present, utterly form'd, impell'd by the past.

The present is to Whitman so self-evidently the focal point of all time that he does not pause to argue its dominance. Instead, he takes the present for granted; he lives chiefly in it and writes most often of it.

Looking into the future, Whitman experiences neither fear nor doubt.

Have you feared that the future would be nothing
    to you?
Is today nothing? Is the beginningless past nothing?
If the future is nothing, they are just as surely noth-
    ing.

He possesses vast patience; he does not expect to cross over Jordan or enter the Promised Land; he is content to believe that the long cycles of time will bridge the gap between his good but imperfect present and an infinitely better future. "A few quadrillions of eras, a few octillions of cubic leagues do not hazard the span or make it impatient." And when, after quadrillions of eras, the future arrives, it will fulfill man's hope.

When Whitman wrote *Leaves of Grass,* he was still so close to the brave days of 1848 that he employed the extravagant language of the new gospel of progress. During the last seventy-five years, the pressures alike of the new science and of world events have led scientists, both social and natural, to abandon the word *progress* for the word *growth* and that, in turn, for *change*. Were Whitman, that persistent reconciler of opposites, with us now he would doubtless transform his romantic concept of progress into something more acceptable to scientists and to historians. Today American Studies are using the resources of the new learning to bridge past and future, in terms which both the historian and the scientist can accept.

After the coming of civilization, a degree of social change which would have required fifty thousand years in prehistory was accomplished within a century. Now it is effected within a decade. This intensified tempo of change sweeps too many of us into the future before we have discovered that the present has become the past. In such days, therefore, we must ask ourselves frequently and searchingly: Which is our tense?

That able spokesman for the past, Mark Van Doren, appears to argue for the continuity of time in the early chapters of his *Liberal Education.* "The completely educated person," he remarks, "is one . . . who has settled some sort of relation in his mind between past, present, and future." To embody that relation, he chooses an appropriate symbol of movement: "The educated person recognizes no dry stretch between now and then. They are one river." And Mr. Van Doren appears to believe that for us ultimate reality is to be

4

found in our own day, when he quotes with approval Whitehead's dictum: "The present contains all there is." But Mr. Van Doren recants in a later chapter where he declares: "Greek literature is not everything, yet it is the heart of what we need to know, along with Roman literature, its derivative." Greek and Latin authors have given us "an account of the world, the clearest and grandest that we have." When we read the ancients, we should remember that the settings of their lives and of ours are "substantially the same," and that truth for them is truth for us.

On this return to the past Mr. Van Doren builds his theory of education. "The medium of liberal education," he declares, "is that portion of the past which is always present" — but nothing of the present not found in the past. He then proposes, as his culminating "Idea of a College," a revival of the medieval trivium and quadrivium and a curriculum of great books in one tense. This belief that truth has once for all been delivered to mankind is shared by the Adler-Hutchins group at the University of Chicago (but not by the majority of their colleagues) and by traditionalists in all parts of the country. Typical is the statement by Norman Foerster that American education must limit itself to "the abiding truths which make the distinction between past and present unimportant."

While past-minded educators thus attempt to stop the clock, the American people move with ever-increasing momentum into a new age. During the half-century since our most venerable professors were freshmen, the United States has more than doubled its population. Where three-fourths of us were rural, three-fifths are now urban. We have harnessed the natural sciences to transform a simple type of industry into a wonder-world of technology. We have pyramided small business into big until our wealth has trebled, and we have become banker to the world. We have shaped a new psychology and a new sociology. We are reconstructing our economics and our political science to fit a society no longer predominantly agrarian but industrial-mercantile-financial-agrarian. We suspect that we should reconstruct our ethics. We have learned to write our own literature. We are learning to paint, dance, compose music, build homes and offices and communities — all in the American idiom. Now in the 1940's, to give final punctuation to this notice that the past is indeed the past, comes the atomic bomb.

A century ago few Americans except poets and philosophers like Whitman and Emerson were insisting that the ideas of an older age do not fit one's own. But today even our businessmen are coming to recognize the same truth, and the president of a large corporation declares of America: "Its men and women must change their habits of thought. . . . Either they meet their new world with new thinking, or they go under." The same pressure is forcing our colleges to put into execution four familiar principles which many of us have accepted in theory but forgotten in practice:

That authority (or the codified experience of the past) has validity for the present only as it is confirmed by the experience of the present;

That the central tense for education is our tense, the present;

That a major function of education is to synthesize the relevant experience of yesterday with that of today;

That reconciliation must be effected between past-minded colleges and a present-minded public.

Whitman was too busy with the common man to take stock of the colleges, but his great ally Emerson gave them his close attention. (What a professor of the humanities Emerson would have been!) "The college, the school of art," he concluded a century ago, "pin me down. They look backward and not forward." (Which helps explain why Harvard never offered him a professorship.) In the middle of the twentieth century we in turn are taking stock of the colleges and of their interpretation of the tenses.

6

For such stock taking it is useful to separate the academic disciplines into three great divisions. The social sciences are the disciplines which deal with both facts and values, the humanities are concerned chiefly with values, and the natural sciences are concerned chiefly but not wholly with facts. In such a classification, history when it deals with values falls among the humanities, and among the social sciences when it deals with facts. It is therefore a bridge between the two groups of disciplines and will be so considered in this discussion. When we call the roll of the social sciences, we find that their dominant tense is inevitably the present. We find, however, that many social scientists accept both past and present and that others are moving in the same direction.

Political Science. Today a well-balanced department of political science gives its first attention to the theory and the contemporary practice of government, of politics, of administration, and in some instances of international law. But it also looks into the past history of political thought, of international organization, of the American constitution, American parties, and American democracy.

Economics. Every department of economics deals in contemporary terms with public finance and international trade, and in generalized terms with economic and monetary theory. Broadly humane departments deal also with economic history, both European and American, and with the history (in addition to the theory) of labor and industry.

Sociology. Social theory, social psychology, and social pathology frequently keep sociologists busy within the present. But the problems of social change lead them back into the history of world migration, of rural and urban society, and of minorities in the United States. Occasionally, however, a man escapes from both tenses into the mere amassing of data as ends in themselves. Here he forgets, like the humanist who mistakes language for one of the humanities rather than their instrument, that statistics are merely tools

7

of the sciences. (This is not to minimize the fact that the statistical method makes possible the social and natural science of our day.)

When we turn to the humanities, we find that from the very nature of their subject matter they are more often backward looking than forward looking. We find also that teachers of the humanities are moving steadily toward that reconciliation of *then* and *now* which makes the future possible.

History. As a discipline which stands among both the social sciences and the humanities, history might perhaps be expected to deal evenhandedly with past and present, but by definition and by common usage, history is a branch of knowledge which deals with the past. And historians themselves, everyone has observed, often gravitate toward the distant rather than the recent past. Where John Citizen knows little American and less ancient history, a narrowly specialized historian may know much about antiquity and nothing about America, for the conditions of his rigorous discipline are calculated to train him as a chronologist of yesterday rather than as an interpreter of today. On the other hand, vital teachers have always been able to transform valleys of dead men's bones into a relevant past — a transformation also accomplished by curriculums in the civilization of the Far East, England, Latin America, the United States. Since history lives in time, here obviously is an essential element in any program which recognizes the tenses. But the historians, if they are to share fully in such a program, must consider not only the Roman Empire but the final hours of yesterday in the United States.

Philosophy and Fine Arts. While many professors of philosophy live in the truth of the past rather than in the truth of both past and present, others apply their knowledge of the ancients to everyday logic and ethics, philosophy in literature, social philosophy, contemporary European thought, and American philosophy. Teachers of art who cannot escape from the aristocratic tradition of beauty for the few find meaning only in baroque architecture or classic ballet. Others recognize not only the major significance of Bach and Rembrandt but the minor yet equally real significance of folk music and jazz, George Bellows and Thomas Hart Benton, and Martha Graham.

Literature. The study of literature must be in the main retrospective. Too many individual teachers, however, are excessively critical of the present. Rejecting general usage for academic jargon, they define "modern" literature as whatever has been written since the Middle Ages and "contemporary" as what their own professors read as students. (In 1936 the late James Wallace, former professor of Greek and early English literature, president of a college, and father of DeWitt Wallace of the *Reader's Digest,* said: "Do you know that I haven't read more than ten of the modern novelists — Scott, Dickens, and the rest? Sounds a bit funny, doesn't it, for a man who is supposed to be educated?") On the other hand, most departments of English keep open their lines of communication between yesterday and today through courses which follow literary types through the centuries and by sequences of courses which bring literary history down to our own day. And an increasing number of institutions accept their responsibility for guiding young writers who are creating the literature of the future.

When we turn from the social sciences and the humanities to the natural sciences we find that, since they are concerned with facts rather than values, the scientist usually operates outside time in a generalized present. On occasion, however, natural scientists place hypotheses (as that of biological evolution) or scientific data in their chronological relationships. When the findings are localized within the United States, the result is instruction in American anthropology, including the culture of the North American Indian, and in the historical geology and historical geography of North America and the regions of the United States. And in the future we may expect to see natural science cooperating with the humanities in exploring the history of science and technology in the United States and in utilizing psychology for the fuller understanding of literature and art in the American past and the American present.

This review of the academic disciplines makes it evident that students and teachers in each of the several humanities have many opportunities to disappear into the past, and we know from personal observation that they do thus escape. Social scientists likewise can and often do live within one tense. In this situation, departmental courses which operate in two tenses (such as have already been cited) are highly useful. But they alone are inadequate to refute the fallacy that *was* and *is* are the same. Well-meaning teachers still insist that there is no boundary between past and present, unaware that they are tacitly committing themselves to the doctrine that time is identical rather than continuous. From such doctrines comes the belief that man's knowledge does not grow or his resources expand, that he lives in a world immutably fixed not in many but in all of its aspects.

It should now be clear that our long-established courses and curriculums in the social sciences (dealing chiefly with the present) and those in the humanities (dealing predominantly with the past) can profitably be supplemented but in no sense supplanted by new curriculums and new courses which synthesize past and present as do American Studies. Essential in any such undertaking are the two academic disciplines in which the past is most important, history and literature. But if a program is to unite the tenses completely, it cannot safely be centered in either or both of these departments, for such a curriculum will be so weighted that it may eventually become retrospective. Neither, for the opposite reason, can it be centered in the social sciences. Rather it must strike a balance between all the relevant humanities and all the relevant social sciences.

TIME AND THE COLLEGES

"I accept Time absolutely." Thus Whitman. And:

The law of the past cannot be eluded,
The law of the present and the future cannot be eluded.
The law of the living cannot be eluded, it is eternal.

In Whitman's view, every college and university should link "the beginningless past" with "the years of the unperform'd." And every curriculum and every course which recognizes that the law of the tenses cannot be eluded and that the law of the present is eternal becomes "an acme of things accomplish'd" and "an encloser of things to come."

II

General Education

As THE need for modifying man's age-old tendency to live in one tense is an essential factor in the making of American Studies, so general education gives contemporary impetus to American programs. General education is a fluid, ever-changing pattern for learning which has emerged during recent decades and is still emerging in American schools and colleges — a pattern for education in the common heritage and the common experience of Americans as free individuals and as citizens in a democratic society. There are three aspects of general education today, not all of them equally relevant to American Studies. General education is, first, generalized rather than specialized — education nearer to that envisioned by Franklin and Rush in eighteenth-century America than by many a young doctor of philosophy fresh from the graduate school in the twentieth century. It is, second, higher education for the many as well as for the few — a new and not universally accepted idea. And it is, third, education which goes beyond the established academic areas into the field of personal living — marriage and parenthood, the use of leisure, and the like. The first aspect of general education is central to American Studies, for one of their major purposes is to generalize knowledge. The second aspect, education for the many, is also relevant; although American Studies are definitely not a program for all students, they are one among the increasing number of curriculums from which each student chooses that most profitable to himself. As courses in personal living contribute

12

only indirectly to American Studies, that area of general education will not be given further consideration here. It must be added, and with emphasis, that general education in American culture does not supplant specialism but draws on it for the materials of synthesis. Nor does general education for the many interfere with education for the few; American Studies are among the opportunities open both to the few and to the many.

This dual movement toward generalizing knowledge and making knowledge more widely available is best understood against the background of history. We recall that education in ancient Greece was education for the very, very few – a handful of free men in the midst of a slave state. In medieval Europe education was for the very few – a little group of men training for religious orders in a feudal state. Their curriculum was inherited from the ancients. During the Renaissance higher education was for the few – gentlemen and commoners training for the learned professions. Their curriculum was handed down through the Middle Ages from the ancients. College education during the early years of the American republic was still restricted to the same two groups and the curriculum was based on the medieval trivium and quadrivium, imitated from the British universities of that day. Concerning the status of these institutions James Conant recently said that in the early nineteenth century "a corrupt sleep hung heavy over the English and Scottish centers of learning."

Thus a relatively static curriculum was offered, century after century, to a slowly growing and yet a definitely growing body of students. In early nineteenth-century America the discrepancy between students and their studies became so acute that Harvard, followed by the lesser New England colleges, imposed on its students a rigorous penal code (chiefly of fines) designed to hold lively boys to the traditional but now barren routine. When a youngster found medievalism unendurable, he could choose an escape to fit

13

his purse. For two cents he could leave morning chapel without due cause; for four cents, absent himself entirely from morning chapel; for six cents, absent himself from class; for seventeen cents, keep a firearm; for fifty cents, use his firearm, absent himself from Sunday chapel, have his hair cut on Sunday, drink liquor, or play cards (this was the fine paid by Nathaniel Hawthorne as a freshman at Bowdoin College when he was caught at the card table); for one dollar, frequent a tippling house or a house of ill fame, indulge in indecent noises on the campus, or attend a stage play — and onward to the final penalty of expulsion, for which price a student could duel, forge, blaspheme, fornicate, assault a tutor or the president of the college, or break his doors or windows.

The boys who became America's first generation of notable authors had little appetite for this regimentation. Bryant entered Williams College at fifteen as a sophomore, but before the year was out he left in disgust. Cooper entered Yale at fourteen with a good grounding in the classics, loafed as a freshman and sophomore, and was expelled as a junior. Irving cast an eye on Columbia College and decided to avoid it on the ground that his health was too frail to support him in the classroom — a correct conclusion based on the wrong reason.

Of the influences which operated in American colleges and universities from those not-too-happy days to the year 1900, five forces were particularly influential, either in a positive or a negative fashion, on the development of general education. All five are known to all of us, but they are commonly evaluated piecemeal rather than as a whole. A brief review of their history will point up their total significance today.

The Expanding Curriculum. The trivium and the quadrivium, which had lingered on in the colonial colleges (and still linger, even today, in a few corners of the academic world), were modified beyond recognition or abandoned

14

entirely. For them the colleges substituted an ever-expanding curriculum, designed to keep abreast of the ever-growing sum of human knowledge. With this encouragement science found it safe to lay aside its disguise as "natural philosophy" and to take its place on the campus in its own name and of its own right, as did also history, economics, and the modern languages. Last of all to be admitted were courses on American subjects, barred from the curriculum until the United States had time to accumulate a past.

Inasmuch as general education recognizes the diversity of human experience, it is committed, at least in theory, to an expanding curriculum. It is true that a college with limited funds must of necessity choose and thereby limit the courses which it offers. It is true also that in the curriculum of any great university there are trivial courses which have no excuse for existence. But any university which appears to offer too many courses actually does not; it offers unnecessary courses. For every futile course which should be omitted, there is an unexplored area in which instruction might well be given.

In practice, general education sets up courses designed to give students an overview of human experience in broad terms. Then administrators, to finance these innovations, sometimes make reductions elsewhere, perhaps in tutorial instruction or in departmental offerings which have been synthesized in the new offerings. Such a reduction is defensible only if there is no net loss in an institution's total coverage of human experience. The curriculum, regardless of the manner in which it is broken down into hours and credits, must grow with a changing world.

The Elective System. The expanding curriculum forced colleges to abandon medieval prescription and to adopt some form of the elective system. Its first distinguished advocate was Thomas Jefferson, who announced the right of election for all men in the Declaration of Independence and later insisted that free election was also the inalienable right of every undergraduate at the University of Virginia. "I am not fully informed concerning the practices at Harvard," he declared early in the nineteenth century, "but there is one from which we shall certainly vary. . . . That is the holding of the students all to one prescribed course. . . . We shall, on the contrary, allow them uncontrolled choice in the lectures they choose to attend." In this proposal Jefferson was influenced not only by the American search for liberty but by current practice in French universities.

General education is committed to exploration of the diversity of human experience and, in addition, to exposition of its essential unity. Where election is entirely free, students may see only diversity. Where a single curriculum out of the past (perhaps built of great books) is imposed on all, then students are shackled with the pseudo-unity of traditionalism. General education follows a middle course; it provides the largest possible number of curriculums (departmental, interdepartmental, interdivisional) and then permits each student to choose from them the program which best fits his interests, his capacities, and his future activity. Thus each student decides (with guidance, of course) which unity is more relevant for him: the unity of a major sequence within an academic department, or the unity of an interdisciplinary program which follows any one of a wide variety of patterns in human experience, among them the patterns of civilization in Asia, Europe, and the Americas.

Specialization. During the first half of the nineteenth century, George Ticknor of Harvard and scores of other Americans studied in German universities and returned to guide their own students through the intricacies of scholarship in the German manner. The immediate effects were excellent, for our provincial imitation of English education was flabby and sterile. Under the German stimulus intellectual life quickened on American campuses, and the idea of the university as an institution for advanced study was born in the United States.

GENERAL EDUCATION

The rewards of specialized study and research are so evident that no one can justly argue that those activities should be discouraged. But we have all observed that at certain points specialism has degenerated into preoccupation with the trivial. When the academic world is compartmentalized into smaller and smaller segments, it may lose contact with actual life until the specialist in self-justification insists that his particular twig is the entire tree and his tree the forest. By way of corrective to all this, general education attempts to synthesize the disciplines. Freshmen and sophomores are offered an opportunity to enroll in generalized and specialized introductions to knowledge. Juniors and seniors choose either a specialized or a generalized major, then balance their specialized major with general courses or vice versa. For graduate students, there are not only the conventional departmental curriculums but new and flexible programs for the M.A. and the Ph.D. degree, which prepare a man to do interdepartmental research or to teach more than one course and even more than one subject.

While general education thus modifies election and specialization, a few administrators are misinterpreting the doctrine that education must center about the common experience of man and are distorting *general* into *uniform*. They are applying to the curriculum the sonorous but disastrous proposal which Ignazio Silone defends in world thought: "If men are not to massacre each other, they must agree on a certain number of fundamental questions: what is good, what evil; what is true, what false; what is beautiful, what ugly" — rather than learn how to live peacefully in a world in which nations and races can never agree as to what is good or beautiful or true. In academic practice this attitude results in the organization of a few general courses designed to teach what certain professors believe to be the good, the true, or the beautiful, and the imposition of those courses on all students. And if a particular program in general education has particular merit, then all upperclassmen are held

17

to that one program. The net result can be a regimentation of general education as contrary to the American spirit as was the regimentation of liberal education a century ago.

Departmentalism. What specialization is in learning, departmentalism is in educational administration. Departmentalization was of course inevitable on the American campus. In 1800 the staff of a small college often consisted of four men, each teaching not a subject but a class — freshmen, sophomores, juniors, or seniors. By 1850, the expanding curriculum produced departments as an administrative necessity. Thereafter, departmentalism was encouraged by specialization, which in turn was encouraged by the German tradition of scholarship and by the ever-growing American respect for experts.

When each academic department is a sovereign state advancing its autonomous interests without regard for its neighbors, it may achieve temporary success, but its best and ultimate interests are not thus served. And in such a situation general education is difficult, if not impossible, to achieve. General education therefore groups departments in three great divisions and asks them to consider their obligations both inside and outside each division. It also asks each department to provide both introductory and advanced courses for nonmajors as well as majors, to lend staff members to other departments, and to cooperate with its neighbors in conducting generalized courses and in shaping over-all policies. A department is enriched rather than impoverished if it sometimes surrenders a potential major student to an interdepartmental curriculum and in return gains for its classes students experienced in the interdisciplinary approach. Likewise, staff members loaned by a department to share in interdepartmental courses find the experience definitely challenging and equally rewarding.

Christian Gauss, dean emeritus of Princeton, is in disagreement with many of us when he announces that America does not need "more research into democracy." We endorse him enthusiastically, however, when he goes on to say that the most important responsibility of teachers is to publish the truth; that "the most effective way of publishing the truths of democracy is to put them into practice"; and that the surest way of practicing them is for teachers "to live and work cooperatively with all other men, above all, with their students." As Mr. Gauss specifically approves of general education, he must, if he is logical, include among "all other men" not only students but a teacher's colleagues in other disciplines with whom the teacher works in any interdepartmental program. That too is one aspect of academic democracy.

The Scientific Method. By 1900 that Johnny-come-lately, natural science, had come into its own, and scientific method commanded the respect of the educational world. Scientists were notably successful in marking out their fields of investigation, in setting up techniques and procedures, and in making specific announcement of their findings. In short, they gave every evidence of knowing where they were going and of knowing how to get there. As the years passed, the scientific method was therefore coveted as well as respected by other disciplines.

Today the vogue of that method is so great that the social scientist often forgets that he may properly give thought to values as well as to facts. Likewise, we in the humanities sometimes attempt to treat values as though they, too, were facts (which is not to deny that, in one meaning of the word, a "value" may indeed be a fact). The divisional organization of learning reminds us that, as there are three tenses, so there are three great areas of knowledge, not one, and that the social sciences and likewise the humanities must stand on their own feet.

These are the major situations and trends which appeared in education during the nineteenth century and these are the modifications which general education has attempted to impose on them. During the present century these problems have been sharply intensified by a sixth factor, a swiftly expanding student population. From 1900 to 1947, the population of the United States increased from 76,000,000 to 139,000,000; that is to say it nearly doubled. Meanwhile the total number of students in college grew from 237,000 to more than 2,250,000; in other words, it increased tenfold. Over a period of forty-seven years, then, the percentage of the total population who go to college and university has expanded fivefold. This means that on an average our colleges and universities enrolled during each of the five decades of this century a new segment of the population as large as the entire segment who went to college in 1900. (Actually, of course, the increment has been proportionately much greater since World War II.)

Traditionalists in America are protesting that "the unfit are coming to college" and are urging that entrance requirements be raised until the four out of five who in 1900 did not enter college but who now do, shall be barred from the campus. A more generous-minded educator in England remarks: "If the United States is making the mistake of giving university education to too many students, it is surely one of the noblest mistakes in history." General education says that it is no mistake, for general education is dedicated to the proposition that all men are entitled to education — not the imposition of one education on all but the provision of an appropriate education for each. And that provision must always include superior curriculums for the superior as well as simplified curriculums for the simple. This second need can be met by our universities and likewise by Vassar, Kenyon, Carleton, Mills, and similar colleges of the liberal arts — if they will educate not for leadership but for leadership in a democracy.

In so far as the formal education of 1900 survives in our classrooms today, the five segments of the American people now in college find its traditional curriculum even more inadequate than did the one segment of our population who went to college in 1900. Nor can the formal education of that day still be relevant in a world turned upside down during the last fifty years by the brilliant and terrifying achievements of the new physics, the new astronomy, the new biology, and the new psychology. When we look about for approaches to learning appropriate to this new age, we find that during this same half-century a few great teachers were training a few students in one or another variety of generalized education. And now for the two and a quarter million, our colleges and graduate schools are breaking down the barriers between academic disciplines and are opening to all the broad highways to learning hitherto known only by the fortunate handful who worked with those pioneer teachers, the great generalizers of the last fifty years. A brief review of the work of a few such teachers will help us to understand general education.

Natural scientists, as they deal with relatively tractable facts, have been (and still are) more successful in coordinating several disciplines than are students of the humanities as they deal with less tractable values. Even as early as the 1870's Willard Gibbs of Yale achieved a memorable union between the two disciplines of physics and mathematics, incomprehensible to his departmentalized colleagues and to all but a half-dozen of his students but illuminating to our scientists today. Within the last half-century Franz Boas of the Field Museum of Natural History and Columbia used anthropology to elucidate history, and Ellsworth Huntington of Yale brought his knowledge of geography to bear on geology, biology, agriculture, economics, and sociology (*Civilization and Climate*, 1915). A Nobel prize has been awarded for the broad research of Joseph Erlanger of Washington University in the two fields of physiology and physics (*Electric Signs of Nervous Activity*, with H. S. Gassner, 1937). And Irving Langmuir of the General Electric Company (no university, of course, yet highly influential on contemporary research) is likewise a Nobel prize winner who

AMERICAN STUDIES

has explored more than one field of science and has also put his discoveries to work for the public.

Among the social scientists, Thorstein Veblen of Chicago and the New School for Social Research guided his students through not only the economics but the sociology and the psychology of Americans (*Theory of the Leisure Class*, 1899, and so forth). Charles Horton Cooley of Michigan (*Human Nature and the Social Order*, 1909) carried on the teaching of social psychology initiated by Veblen. Carleton Parker of the University of Washington suggested how psychology may contribute to the study of economics, particularly to the economics of American labor.

Even though William James of Harvard taught psychology and philosophy when the former was still catalogued as a subdivision of the latter (a survival of the generalized education of the age of Franklin), his pupils found in him a master of synthesis (*Psychology*, 1890; *The Varieties of Religious Experience*, 1902). So did the pupils of a second great psychologist-philosopher, John Dewey of Columbia and the New School (*School and Society*, 1899). Both men, we should not forget, drew heavily on American sources and contributed substantially to American thought.

The first distinguished student of our native literature, Moses Coit Tyler (*A History of American Literature, 1607-1765*, 1878), held an interdisciplinary position as professor of American literature and history at Cornell. Today *Main Currents in American Thought* (1927-30), by Vernon L. Parrington of the University of Washington, is still used as a text in three departments: political science, history, and literature. (Only death prevented Parrington from completing his study of American ideas in the present tense.) When we have learned how to use psychology in the study of literature, we shall respect Ludwig Lewisohn for his unsuccessful yet forward-looking attempt in that direction (*Expression in America*, 1932).

In 1893 Frederick Jackson Turner, then of Wisconsin and

22

later of Harvard, read his famous paper on "The Significance of the Frontier in American History" and won the enmity of narrow departmentalists in at least five fields: geography, political science, sociology, economics, and history. James Harvey Robinson of Columbia promoted the new history, in which his pupils synthesized the findings of anthropologists, psychologists, economists, sociologists, and historians. And Charles A. Beard of Columbia and the New School trained scholars not only in American history but in economics and political science (*Economic Interpretation of the Constitution of the United States*, 1913; *The Rise of American Civilization*, with Mary Beard, 1927).

Out of such teaching there developed before World War II a variety of generalized curriculums: comparative literature, comparative philology, the history of science, the history and the philosophy of religion, regional planning, public administration, international relations, genetics, statistics, and the civilization of an epoch or an area (the Middle Ages, the Renaissance, the Enlightenment, the Far East, the Near East, England, France, Latin America, the United States).

The directions in which general education has moved are suggested by two undertakings at Minnesota. In 1932 that university instituted a General College designed to carry out both aims of general education, that is, to synthesize knowledge and to provide higher education for a larger percentage of the population — in this instance, for those who, if they enter a four-year liberal arts college, are likely to leave before graduating. In its two-year curriculum a variety of courses are offered, certain of them modified from departmental courses and others developed specifically for the General College. The second undertaking is the more recent department of general studies in the liberal arts college, designed to provide generalized courses for students who are capable of taking (and in most instances will take) the B.A. degree and to whom specialized education is already available. These general studies provide guidance in personal living and surveys of the natural sciences, the social sciences, and the humanities. Minnesota, it should be observed, is careful to examine the humanities not only in the past but in the present tense, through a sequence of interdepartmental courses in the European heritage, the humanities in modern Europe, and American life.

The actualities of World War II made many professors and many students dissatisfied with the more restricted varieties of academic specialism, and eager to grapple with knowledge in more inclusive terms; the equally bitter actualities of the postwar years have increased that dissatisfaction and that eagerness. The trend away from departmentalization and toward more general curriculums thus takes on ever-increasing momentum as a variety of new interdisciplinary programs appear. In 1945, public attention was focused on these developments by a useful restatement of the principles of general education by Harvard University in *General Education in a Free Society.* Harvard is now putting these principles into execution by adding to its curriculum several of the new general-studies courses.

Stimulating also is the series of curriculums (old and new) now open to undergraduates at Yale. In the category of field majors are included American studies, Latin American affairs, Russian studies, Chinese studies, Japanese studies, and history, the arts, and letters. Described as interdepartmental majors are French and philosophy, mathematics and philosophy, physics and philosophy, and the Scholars-of-the-House program. In the category of divisional programs in general studies are literature, philosophy, and the arts; the arts and criticism; religious and ethical thought; history, politics, and economics; social science and literature; social science and philosophy; social science and psychology; society, psychology, and literature.

Still something of an experiment, general education has nevertheless operated long enough to prove that we must not reject the possibility of any transfer of learning except in identical elements. We have learned instead that wherever the method of learning encourages generalization, the learner takes away not only specific information but also an increased capacity for generalizing — a capacity which he can use in new situations. We have learned also that students who specialize in college are no more successful in graduate or professional schools than are broadly educated students, and that what matters is not the acquisition of specific information but the development of sound habits in studying and in thinking. As we generalize, we learn.

III

American Studies

BECAUSE programs in American civilization have sometimes been set up independently and sometimes as part of a broader curriculum, it is difficult to say exactly when and where the first was initiated. In the early 1930's (when general education was getting under way) Harvard and Yale encouraged joint study in history and literature, permitting students to concentrate in various areas, of which one was American culture. By 1939 either graduate or undergraduate programs in American civilization were offered by Pennsylvania, Chicago, Amherst, Smith, and George Washington. During the war the rate of increase in such curriculums fell off slightly. Since the war existing programs have been revived, new programs have been organized with increasing frequency (in 1945-46, for example, more than a dozen were introduced), and more are projected. In the academic year 1947-48, more than sixty institutions offered the B.A. degree in American civilization, and approximately fifteen offered the M.A. degree or the Ph.D. degree or both.

Further indications of substantial interest in American Studies are programs devoted to that subject at the annual meetings of the American Historical Association and the Modern Language Association, a Committee on American Civilization set up by the American Literature Group of the Modern Language Association and a second by the National Council of Teachers of English, fellowships for the interdisciplinary study of American culture granted by the American Council of Learned Societies, a Committee on American

Civilization appointed by that council, a postdoctoral fellowship for study of undergraduate programs in American civilization to be awarded for 1949-51 by the University of Pennsylvania, and a journal of American Studies to be inaugurated in 1949 by the University of Minnesota. Various fellowships are offered by universities and foundations for the study of American history and culture, and grants are available from scholarly foundations. American Studies, it is evident, have been established long enough and accepted widely enough to permit generalization concerning them.

For synthesizing past with present and for charting possible futures, American Studies are only one of many appropriate fields in modern education. But in American colleges and universities today our own is the civilization which offers students the widest resources by way of books published, scholars trained, and courses taught. In fact American courses, of which examples are cited in Chapter V, are *in toto* so numerous and so diversified that the problem is often not to find sufficient material for an American program but to determine what shall be omitted. When we also recall that our culture has a highly usable past, a notable present, and better prospects for the future than are granted to any other civilization in this epoch of uncertainty, we conclude that no other curriculum offers better opportunity for uniting the tenses.

For synthesizing the departmental disciplines included in the divisions of the social sciences and the humanities, American Studies are again only one of many appropriate curriculums, but again they are one of the most effective. The fashion in which various departments contribute to American Studies has already been suggested, and further details are presented in the next two chapters. These details make it clear that, even though American Studies and general education have usually developed independently and though educators do not always associate the two, American Studies are a thoroughgoing exemplification of general education as it is interpreted in this volume. And no other curriculum offers fuller opportunity for balancing education in facts with education in values.

Although undergraduate training in American civilization should be suitable preparation both for living and for earning, at the moment it is in practice nonvocational only. Students who propose to enter a profession with only the bachelor's degree are forced to take a specialized training in their chosen field: journalism, social work, business administration, teaching, or the like. The secondary-school system is still so departmentalized that it usually will not license graduates in American Studies to teach American history, civics, or literature; rather students must meet departmental requirements in social studies or English. In the future (when the current shortage of secondary-school teachers is relieved) it is probable that five-year curriculums for the B.S. in education will be established, permitting one major in a department in which teachers' certificates are issued (for example, history or social studies, English, art) supported by a second major in American Studies. Broad knowledge of one's own civilization will then have cash as well as cultural value — and the disastrous assumption that education for earning and for living cannot be combined will again be refuted in concrete terms. But at present only a small percentage of students who must earn their own living can afford to pursue this nonvocational program, as compared with students who have independent incomes.

Graduate training in American Studies, on the other hand, is at once a nonvocational education in the unity of time and of the academic disciplines, and a professional training for a variety of careers. Men and women who have taken or are taking advanced degrees in American Studies are engaged in or preparing for social work, government service, reporting and editing both for the press and for radio, book reviewing, library work, creative writing, and teaching — most

frequently the teaching of history, literature, or American
Studies. As individuals who take the M.A. or the Ph.D. degree in an interdepartmental curriculum in American civilization commonly have either a lower degree or an equivalent training in a departmental discipline, colleges are usually willing to give them departmental appointments. As
American Studies become better known, additional positions will doubtless be open to students trained in the new
curriculum — on the staffs of historical societies, for instance,
and of magazine and book publishers.

American Studies are not appropriate to all students. If
an undergraduate asks for admission to an American program because he is interested in the technique of one of the
arts in the United States, he should be directed into a major
in the appropriate department. If he is deeply interested in
the past and present of the United States but insists on con-
fining himself to the chronological approach, he should be
directed into the department of history (which is not to sug-
gest that historians do not deal with ideas). If he is a graduate student who seeks to take a degree in American literature without meeting the requirements of the department of
English, he should be sent back to that department. But if
he is concerned with the broad outlines of knowledge, with
the relationships between the humanities and the social sciences, or with the pattern of American life, or if he already
has a specialized training which needs enrichment, then
American Studies are his field.

Any program, undergraduate or graduate, which is based
on the heritage and the environment of the student himself
has unique weakness, both actual and fancied, against which
the student must be protected. A mediocre student, for example, who has no interest in any departmental discipline
(such a lack is not of necessity discreditable) occasionally
drifts into American Studies on the assumption that since he
is an American, he will find American subjects easy. He is
soon disillusioned, for he is placed in competition with de-

partmental majors in departmental courses where he cannot succeed unless he possesses both intellectual capacity and a substantial knowledge of American culture, in lieu of specialized knowledge within several departments. If these students become a problem, they can usually be barred from American Studies by rejecting, as several institutions now do, all candidates for the program who do not attain a specified degree of distinction as freshmen and sophomores.

Excessive immediacy is often charged against such programs as American Studies (as it is, perhaps with more justice, against American education in general). This immediacy takes the form of disregard, first, of indirect expression, symbol, and form and, second, of tradition and the past. It is, we are told, a barbarian's insistence on "seeing things as they are" — that is, directly and in the present. Students of American culture are protected from both these errors in every balanced (that is to say, thoroughly interdisciplinary) American program which deals with form in our arts and with the history of our past. But any program in which students can avoid all the arts (including literature) and/or history is guilty of one or both of these forms of immediacy.

In the United States any program which concerns the students themselves may become or, more likely, be accused of being chauvinistic. In England and on the continent it is taken for granted that a student will normally be best informed concerning his own literature and the other aspects of his own culture, but certain Americans still exhibit an inverted provincialism which either denies that we have developed a culture or dismisses it as crudely immature. The actual situation today is quite otherwise. Where American culture was once adolescent and European cultures were adult, the former has now passed into early maturity and the latter (with the exception of Russian civilization) have passed into late maturity. There are available, therefore, diversified and distinguished materials for American programs in which there need be neither parochialism nor chauvinism.

Granted that such materials exist, we must still be careful not to misuse them. To provide students with a basis for judging American culture several institutions require them to include courses on some aspect of foreign civilization in their major concentration or in a minor. As a major program rarely occupies more than half of an undergraduate's time in the junior and senior years, he can minor in a foreign area and still have room for free electives. It is not always practical to include such a requirement in the single year of study for the M.A. degree, but in most universities candidates for the Ph.D. are required to study a foreign civilization.

There is no danger that the teaching staff in American Studies will become chauvinists as long as two conditions are maintained. First, the faculty should continue to be distributed, as at present, in several departments, where they teach non-American as well as American courses or are closely associated with teachers who do. An interdivisional group of six to a dozen men in a small college, or forty to fifty in a large university, will not turn to chauvinism until the institution itself runs mad. If independent departments of American civilization are set up, each with its own staff, there is a possibility but no necessity that they might eventually become excessively nationalistic. But when and if American Studies become departmentalized, they will have lost one of the major reasons for their existence.

Second, the teaching and likewise the administration of American Studies should remain in the hands of men who believe that isolation makes world peace impossible as surely as selfish sectionalism makes national unity impossible, and who are convinced also that as healthy regional loyalty strengthens loyalty to the United States, so sane national patriotism contributes to the building of a world society. These relationships are, in fact, so important to American Studies that the final chapter in this volume is devoted to a consideration of "Region, Nation, World."

Over against these weaknesses (real, potential, and imagined) must be set the unique strengths of a curriculum which deals with the students' native culture. There is, of course, the initial and obvious advantage that students bring with them a certain amount of information concerning the United States — enough, at least, to let them move from the known to the unknown without a preliminary briefing in a foreign civilization. And their personal knowledge of regional, vocational, racial, religious, and similar elements in American life enriches classroom discussion and their entire program. (It is no accident that teachers who cooperate with each other in interdepartmental programs usually reject the motto, "The student does not tell me; I tell him," and draw information from their students as well as give it to them.)

There is the equally obvious advantage that what students take from their American Studies has close relevance to their living, both on the campus and later in public life. An undergraduate who majors in American civilization spends his junior and senior years not in the isolation of an ivied tower but in the stream of human experience. And a graduate student of American culture can, without surrendering to gross immediacy, remain a citizen while he is a scholar. Nowhere in the liberal arts is there a better hope than in American Studies for bridging the unnatural gulf which separates the campus from the world outside.

American Studies are unique, finally, in their discipline. It should be said at once that this is not an academic discipline as that concept has come down to us from the Middle Ages. It should also be said that when and if such an academic discipline takes form in American Studies, they will have become specialized and we shall be forced to find a new approach to our national culture. This is not to damn specialization; it is merely to remark that any program set up to supplement specialism must of necessity avoid it.

This new discipline is shaped by a conception known to numerous peoples but peculiarly welcome to Americans —

the belief that we must accept both the diversity and the unity of life and then resolve them. In the words of the founding fathers, *E pluribus unum.* In the terms of economics and politics today, the claims of the single individual must be reconciled with those of a democratic society. In the words of Whitman,

> One's-self I sing — a simple, separate Person;
> Yet utter the word Democratic, the word *En-masse.*

When the idea of unity within diversity is translated into the modest terms of the procedures of American Studies, it is not reduced to triviality but takes on concrete relevance. The discipline of American Studies is the intellectual process whereby a student assimilates the complicated and often contradictory details of American civilization which he meets in his courses in social science, history, literature, philosophy, and the fine arts. And it is the intellectual process whereby he fashions out of them a picture of these United States. In so doing, he reduces diversity to some degree of unity.

The techniques which a student employs in this synthesis are drawn from departmental disciplines and from his instruction in American Studies. From historians he learns something of their approach to time; from humanists, something of their approach to values; from social scientists, something of their approach to facts and to values. He must have, therefore, the guidance of teachers trained in departmental specialism and of teachers broadly trained in American Studies. But much responsibility rests on the student himself. His is not a traditional approach to an academically devised department, but the pragmatic approach of a free and mature man to the actualities of life. He works, then, in the heritage of Emerson and his philosophy of self-trust and in the heritage of William James and his philosophy of pragmatism.

Since the days when the ancients decided that the seven

liberal arts are grammar, rhetoric, logic, arithmetic, geometry, astronomy, and music, the most revolutionary proposal in education is the current proposal that knowledge be reorganized according to patterns of our own experience. Of the reorganizations now in progress, none has more validity than American Studies — a program directed toward the ultimate goals of charting, evaluating, and perpetuating the pattern (sometimes clear but often confused) of action, thought, and imagination in the United States.

IV

Curriculums in American Studies

No two of the American curriculums which have been established from the University of Maine to the University of California are alike, for each institution has devised a program to fit its own needs and its own resources in American courses. This chapter, then, is not devoted to a search for the perfect plan for American Studies as it exists in the mind either of God or of the committee on American civilization in any university. It is, rather, a survey of the varieties of curriculums which local conditions have produced. And it is assumed that American programs will be best served if each institution informs itself concerning all procedures throughout the country and then adopts those which are relevant to its own aims, with no attempt to achieve uniformity with other programs.

Three conditions are essential for organizing an American curriculum. First there must be enabling legislation or administrative sanction. In numerous liberal arts colleges American programs have been set up under existing provisions for a divisional major, a general education major, a liberal arts major, or the like. In certain graduate schools there are similar provisions but more often specific authorization is required. Interdisciplinary curriculums are always instituted cooperatively by members of more than one department, but in most institutions it is not necessary to ask the departments concerned to vote their formal approval, as the program is directed by a committee responsible not to the heads of departments but to the dean of the college or school.

The second condition is the presence on the faculty of a few individuals who are so deeply concerned with the broad interpretation of American culture that they will take on, in addition to their departmental duties, the guidance of such a program. There must be, further, a staff member or two who will make the advancement and the administration of American Studies their first concern. These men in the past have usually been self-trained in the interdisciplinary approach; in the future they will more often be trained in programs in American civilization. It is evident that a committee on American Studies must and should be composed in the main of men who hold departmental appointments, but it is becoming evident also that, as American programs grow larger, the persons who administer them must be freed from part of their departmental responsibilities. This release is now accomplished by buying part of their time from the departments in which they hold appointment, either by setting up a budget for American Studies or by informal agreement. When the academic world recognizes that American Studies have achieved permanent status, men who direct American programs and interdisciplinary courses will perhaps be given specific appointments in American civilization. But such administrative adjustments will in no sense be equivalent to establishing a department of American civilization. It is pertinent to add that where an American curriculum is set up on paper but enrolls very few or no students, its failure may usually be traced to heavy departmental duties which prevent sympathetic faculty members from supporting the project.

The last condition for initiating an American program is in many instances the easiest of the three to fulfill, for the provision of appropriate courses is usually not difficult even in small colleges with limited resources. All that is required is two or three courses in American history, a course or two in American literature, a few social science courses on American topics, a course in American philosophy, and courses in two or three of these fields: American art, American music, the history of religion in the United States. Even though smaller institutions may consider themselves handicapped in comparison with a large university, their strong liberal arts tradition often gives them a wider distribution of courses, especially in the arts and philosophy (where many universities offer little in American terms). The fact is that suitable courses are now available on almost every campus, ready for integration into an American program.

Various points of view are reflected in the requirements made of freshmen and sophomores who propose to take the B.A. degree in American civilization. At Colgate, for example, underclassmen prepare for American Studies by taking such courses as American Civilization and American Government. At Scripps, on the other hand, they study non-American backgrounds, either in introductory courses in departmental disciplines or in interdepartmental surveys of European civilization. In several colleges underclassmen are required to enroll both in general departmental courses and in American courses. Mills, for example, prescribes a neatly balanced diet of, first, Introduction to the Study of Man, Elements of Sociology, Elements of Economics and, second, American Civilization, Ethnic Groups in the United States, American Constitutional Government. In general, it appears that a considerable proportion of students begin their upperclass study of American civilization without a course in the general history either of Europe or the United States, and a large majority without an interdisciplinary introduction to American culture.

UNDERGRADUATE PROGRAMS

For everyone who is concerned with the new departmentalism, the patterns into which American curriculums fall are significant. There are seven of these general patterns on the undergraduate level. Six of these have been adopted (1947-48) by two to eight colleges each, and the seventh by a majority of the colleges. The three simplest patterns

AMERICAN STUDIES

accomplish many of the ends of interdisciplinary study, while at the same time they meet the major requirements of a single department. A few colleges offer what they describe as a program in American civilization, constituted of a major in English supported by a minor (usually in history) or minors, all with special attention to American courses. A slightly larger number of institutions offer a program made up of a major in history and a minor in English, again with emphasis on American courses. More flexible is the program in a half-dozen colleges in which a student majors in any one of two to six departments but concentrates on American courses in his major and his minor or minors, if any.

The most notable example of this last approach is the undergraduate program in American civilization at Princeton. There a student prepares himself in European civilization as a freshman and then majors in one of six departments (art and archaeology, economics, English, history, philosophy, or politics), with attention both to American civilization and to its backgrounds in Europe. In the sophomore and the junior year (under a revised curriculum effective in 1948) he studies American history, literature or art, philosophy or thought, political science or sociology, and one of the following four special fields: America and western civilization, American social institutions, patterns of ideas, and the creative intelligence. In the junior year he also does independent reading and takes a comprehensive examination; in the senior year he participates in a conference on American civilization (see page 67) and writes his senior thesis. Meanwhile he meets the requirements of his major department and thus is graduated from that department, with a certificate of proficiency in American Studies.

As history and literature bulk large in every American curriculum, several colleges have organized programs calling for a joint major or its equivalent in those two departments. In 1906, for example, a general concentration in history and literature was established in Harvard College under the

38

chairmanship of George Santayana. For more than two decades students were concerned only with foreign studies, but early in the 1930's the first undergraduate took a degree in American civilization within this concentration. The total enrollment in history-literature is now limited to 150 students, of whom approximately one half devote themselves to American Studies. History-literature was the first field at Harvard in which the tutorial method was employed; as all students now accepted for the program are honors students, all are given tutorial guidance. A few institutions which do not offer this same concentration in history and literature have set up independent programs in American civilization built around courses in these departments. Illustrations are the major in American history and literature at Williams and the concentration in American literature and civilization at Northwestern. The latter calls for sixty quarter-hours which must include a continuous year-course in the history of the United States and one in its literature and some work in at least two other related departments, under the direction of an adviser in the department either of English or of history. A course in the history of western civilization is a prerequisite to this program.

Patterns five and six are curriculums administered within the academic division of the social sciences or the division of the humanities. Even though no institution limits students of American civilization to courses in either division, each pattern has the effect of minimizing the significance of the division not specifically included.

The last type of curriculum, that adopted by some thirty institutions, is interdivisional (that is to say, interdisciplinary in the most inclusive sense). Its only significant difference from types four, five, and six is the greater degree to which it ignores departmental and divisional boundaries to link the tenses and to unite the disciplines. Apparently the first independent program in American civilization (as distinct from the history-literature concentration at Harvard) was initiated in Columbian College of George Washington University in 1936-37. From that date to 1947-48 the program has graduated approximately eighty students. This major in American thought and civilization is concerned with four fields: European cultural history, American history, American fine arts, American literature and philosophy. No specific courses are required; students prepare themselves for a general examination (at the end of the senior year) through recommended courses, independent reading, and a proseminar (see page 66). With the cooperation of the professor of American history and other colleagues in related fields, the professor of American literature administers the major, acts as adviser and tutor, conducts the proseminar, and gives the general examination.

A well-distributed interdivisional major is that at Smith College. Students are required to take American courses in history, literature, art or music, and philosophy, education, religion, government, or sociology. The unusual resources of the college in music, art, philosophy, and the history of religion give American Studies a range and a solidity at Smith which they sometimes lack in larger institutions. The major has been directed by a professor of history and by an interdepartmentally trained professor of English who teaches also in the department of government. The committee on American civilization (the director and representatives of the departments in which courses are required) meets frequently to discuss the program. Superior students who take honors in American civilization do directed reading in the second semester of the junior year, write a paper in the first semester of the senior year, take an integrating proseminar in the second semester, and write three examinations: one on American cultural history as a whole, one on concrete interrelationships of two fields in the major, and one on the investigation of specific topics assigned in advance.

The undergraduate program initiated at Yale in 1946-47

is unusual in its emphasis on the socio-anthropological approach to culture. A year's course in American history is a prerequisite; the major is open only to superior students; enrollment is at present limited to twenty-five. In the junior year students take part in a proseminar on techniques in the study of American cultures conducted by men in history, sociology, and literature (see page 66). In addition, students select two one-year courses dealing with American civilization from one of the following groups, and one course from each of the other two: (a) history, government; (b) sociology, anthropology, economics; (c) literature, art, philosophy. Seniors write an essay (which counts as one course) under tutorial guidance on such topics as "A Small Town and Its Merchants," "The Sense of Atlantic City," or "The Symbol of Money in the Novels of Henry James." While the Yale program thus seeks to interpret history and literature not only in their own terms but in those of socio-anthropological culture, anthropologists in various parts of the country are expanding their field of study to include literate as well as primitive society. Out of this cross-fertilization of academic disciplines a new approach to American Studies may emerge.

But these elaborate curriculums for honors students are by no means representative. Most programs in American Studies are conducted by institutions which make no special provisions for graduation with honors; their programs, then, are geared to the interests and the capacities of undergraduates in general. More representative than the curriculums at Princeton, Harvard, and Yale are the programs at George Washington, Northwestern, and Smith (for students who do not take honors). Another well-balanced undergraduate curriculum (now temporarily suspended) is that at Ohio State University: Introduction to Geography, Economic Geography, and Geography of the United States and Canada; History of Western Civilization, History of the United States, and Recent History of the United States; Foreign Governments, American Government; Principles of Economics,

Economic History of the United States; American Literature, The American Renaissance in Literature; History of American Art; a proseminar in American civilization; and thirty additional semester-hours.

It should be added that several curriculums originally conceived in broadly interdepartmental terms, described in college bulletins as such, and listed as such in this tabulation are in practice little more than a major-minor or joint major in history and literature. This situation may be expected to change as men in other disciplines learn more concerning American Studies.

Of the universities which grant advanced degrees in American Studies, one offers only the M.A. (Maine), and five only the Ph.D. (Harvard, Yale, Wisconsin, Texas, New Mexico). Nine have organized curriculums for both degrees: Brown, New York, Pennsylvania, Maryland, George Washington, Ohio State, Western Reserve, Iowa, and Minnesota.* As it is difficult to conduct a graduate program in American civilization within one department, these curriculums are in almost every instance interdepartmental. Exceptions are George Washington (with its unique provisions for graduate study) and Wisconsin. At the former, candidates for the M.A. study in Columbian College in the program in American literary and cultural history, and candidates for the Ph.D. work in the special field of American literary nationalism under a member of the graduate council. Wisconsin offers two separate curriculums: first, the Ph.D. in American culture, administered by men in American literature with the assistance of related departments and calling for knowledge of European literature and culture, two fields of American literature (prior to and since 1836), and courses in two

*These are the fifteen universities from which it was possible to secure information in 1947-48. Although it is possible that advanced degrees are offered elsewhere, it is not likely that data from additional universities would change the general picture presented in this chapter.

or three related fields; and, second, the Ph.D. in American civilization, administered by men in American history with the assistance of related departments and calling for knowledge of European history, three courses in American history, additional courses in related fields, and a double minor.

At Pennsylvania this same distribution is maintained by a committee on American civilization with two chairmen, one responsible for students whose chief interest is in history and social sciences and the other responsible for those in literature, philosophy, and art. Students are required to take a minimum of sixteen credits each in the history and the literature of the United States. Although they are permitted to select courses in American philosophy, art, sociology, education, and economics, students tend to concentrate their attention on either history or literature. The Pennsylvania program stresses both the homogeneity of American civilization and the interrelations between American, British, and Continental history and literature.

The graduate curriculum at Yale was originally a part of the concentration in history, the arts, and letters, where students majored in English studies, medieval studies, or American Studies. The first Ph.D. degree in American civilization in history, the arts, and letters was granted in 1933 (dissertation topic, "The American Cult of Success"). American Studies later became an independent curriculum, which has been directed by a professor of English with the assistance of men in the departments of history, English, government, sociology, economics, and history of art. The only formal requirement at present is a course in historiography and a seminar in American Studies (directed by Yale's first graduate in American civilization, who has won recognition as a teacher of history, of international relations, and of government and as a scholar in the same fields). Most students in the program register for American culture in the department of sociology, a course in American literature in the department of English, and an American Studies course in the history of ideas, and many enroll also in American art. Beyond these courses, students follow their own interests.

Harvard has granted more doctoral degrees than any other university and has probably been more influential on graduate curriculums than any other. Graduate study in American civilization was organized in 1937 as an independent program under the interdivisional Committee on Higher Degrees in the History of American Civilization, while the undergraduate program remains in the history-literature concentration. As suggested by the title of the committee and confirmed by the curriculums outlined below, the approach is historical. Knowledge of at least five of the following subjects is required—including in all cases (1), at least two from (2) to (5), and one chosen from (6) to (13): (1) the social and economic history of the United States, (2) the history of literature in the United States, (3) the history of political and constitutional thought in the United States, (4) the history of religion and theology in the United States, (5) the history of philosophy in the United States, (6) the history of science and learning, (7) the history of the fine arts, (8) the history of religion and theology, (9) the history of philosophy, (10) the history of political theory, (11) the history of education, (12) the history of European literature (especially English), (13) any other subject or subjects, knowledge of which is in the opinion of the committee desirable for the student's successful carrying on of his thesis. Dissertations have been written on these subjects: "American Attitudes toward the West, 1803-50"; "Religion and the Family in Eighteenth-Century America"; "Cincinnati, 1818-38"; "Industrialism in the American Novel, 1814-90"; "New England Popular Tales and Legends"; "Pre-Muckraking in American Fiction, 1870-1901"; "Criticism and the Problem of Literary Expression in a Democratic Society"; "The Quaker Merchants of Philadelphia, 1682-1763"; "Arminianism in Massachusetts, 1735-80"; "The Reception of European Literary Nationalism in the United States, 1870-1900"; and

"Henry B. Fuller and the Chicago Literary Movement." No seminar on American civilization is conducted, but one may develop out of the meetings of a group of graduate students.

Programs created *de novo* rather than adopted from existing concentrations in history-literature draw heavily on those two disciplines, yet tend to utilize more fully the resources of other departments. Such is the case at Ohio State, Western Reserve, and Iowa. Even more thoroughly committed to interdepartmentalism is Chicago. There two general curriculums lead to the M.A. and the Ph.D., one in the history of culture within the Division of the Humanities and the other in social thought within the Division of the Social Sciences. Although American civilization is one of the several fields in both curriculums, students of American life have chosen to enroll in the history of culture. No specific course requirements are set up; an individual program is devised to fit each student. In every instance, the program includes courses in both humanities and social sciences, thus making it interdivisional in practice if not in name.

These formal curriculums take on sharper focus and gain increased momentum wherever institutions capitalize on their local resources. At Brown University the wealth of early Americana in the John Carter Brown Library has already been tapped by the program in American culture, and the Harris Collection of American Poetry and Plays likewise offers unusual opportunity for advanced study. At the University of New Mexico distinguished courses in the archeology, art, and history of the Southwest supply a sound regional core for an American curriculum, and the first doctoral dissertation at Albuquerque was very appropriately concerned with the folklore of the region. The University of Maryland has a unique opportunity for correlating graduate and undergraduate study, as candidates for bachelor's degrees in all colleges and all departments are required to study American civilization, American government, sociology of American life, and readings in American literature (in conjunction with composition). On other campuses, these opportunities have their local parallels.

To supplement existing resources, colleges and universities are making new provisions to meet the needs of these new curriculums. As students of American civilization have no departmental ties, every committee on American Studies finds it necessary to make full provision for counseling, both to help students integrate their courses and to give them a sense of security. It is already evident that a program should enroll only as many students as can be given capable guidance. A further service is the provision of reading lists in American civilization, for candidates both for the bachelor's degree and for advanced degrees.

Informal American Studies clubs have been organized, sometimes by faculties but more often by students. At Harvard, some fifteen advanced students met every other week during 1947-48 in the home of a faculty member, for discussions led by a chairman appointed for each session and recorded by a secretary similarly appointed. The group took De Tocqueville and Bryce as points of departure for outlining a survey of the United States today. Members of the American Studies Club at Pennsylvania drew up plans for a series of lectures; their suggestions were adopted by the university for the Franklin lectures; and five speakers addressed evening audiences of five hundred to a thousand: Brand Blanshard, Yale (philosophy); F. O. Matthiessen, Harvard (literature); Dixon Wecter, Huntington Library (social institutions); Detlov Bronk, Pennsylvania (science); and George F. Thomas, Princeton (religion). On the day following each lecture, the speaker met with the students for discussion. At Yale a club meets one evening a month, calling upon representatives of various disciplines to discuss their approaches to the problems of American civilization.

A symposium on American civilization for students and faculty was sponsored in 1944-45 by the School of Humanities of Stanford University. Among the topics and speakers

were these: "Alexander Wilson and John James Audubon,"
by Frederick O. Koenig (chemistry); "Some Attitudes
toward American Folklore," by Desmond S. Powell (humanities); "Henry George: Democratic Thinker of California,"
by Charles A. Barker (history); "Geology in Relation to the
Settlement of the West," by Bailey Willis (geology); "Contemporary American Painting," by Daniel M. Mendelowitz
(art). An institute in American culture for the general public and for the staff of Roosevelt College and undergraduates
in the program in American culture was conducted in 1945-
46. The subject was the impact of the Midwest on our
national life. Topics and speakers were as follows: literature,
John T. Flanagan (Southern Methodist, now at Illinois);
religious culture, William W. Sweet (Chicago); immigrant
contributions, Carter Davidson (Knox); humor, Walter Blair
(Chicago); liberalism, Walter Johnson (Chicago); language,
S. I. Hayakawa (Illinois Institute of Technology). Other
municipal and state institutions interested in education outside the classroom will doubtless perform a similar public
service by offering lecture and recital series in American
terms.

In Europe, American Studies are pursued at the moment
both in permanent institutes within European universities
and in a summer institute conducted by Americans on a
temporary basis. The latter is the Salzburg seminar in American civilization, initiated by a group of Harvard students
concerned with making an intellectual as well as a material
contribution to the recovery of civilization in Europe. The
first session, in the summer of 1947, was attended by sixty-
seven registrants (graduate students, younger faculty members, and lecturers) from eighteen countries. Subjects and
faculty were as follows: literature, F. O. Matthiessen (Harvard), Vida Ginsberg (New School for Social Research),
and Alfred Kazin; history, Richard Schlatter (Rutgers) and
Elspeth Davis (Sarah Lawrence); government, Benjamin
Wright (Harvard) and Neil McDonald (New Jersey Col-

lege for Women); economics, Wassily Leontief (Harvard) and Walt Rostow (Oxford); sociology, Margaret Mead (American Museum of Natural History); mass communication, Lyman Bryson (Columbia). The institute was so successful in reconciling national antagonisms through free discussion and in training European scholars in the American field that observers hope Salzburg may become a permanent center for American Studies.

The permanent European institutes involve only one or two disciplines, or at most three. The most extensive is that in the University of Upsala under the direction of Professor S. B. Liljegren. There the major interest is "American philology in the wider sense"; some attention is given also to "other subjects connected with the American Humanities." The institute has its own building and its own library and publishes a series of essays and studies on American language and literature. The first five titles deal with American and British pronunciation, John Campanus' Delaware translation of the catechism, Hawthorne and gothic romance, the influence of Zola on Frank Norris, and the revolt against American literary romanticism in S. L. Clemens. Kenneth Murdock (Harvard) and Stanley T. Williams (Yale) have been visiting professors at Upsala. The University of Oslo opened an American institute on January 1, 1948, under the direction of Professor Sigmund Skard. In preparation for his new duties, Professor Skard spent a year in the United States, visiting American programs and collecting a library for the institute. Courses have been given at Oslo from time to time in American literature, history, geography, ethnology, philosophy, and so forth; with the establishment of the institute annual courses in American literature and history are assured. The present function of these institutes and of the chair of American civilization at the Collège de France is not to provide an interdisciplinary program for a degree but to develop instruction in various aspects of American culture within the established academic disciplines and to provide facilities for research.

CURRICULUMS IN AMERICAN STUDIES

Increased interest in the United States among Europeans is reflected in the invitation of I. A. Kandel, editor of *School and Society*, to organize a curriculum in American civilization at the University of Manchester in the spring of 1948 and to fill a chair of American civilization in that university, and is reflected too in the presence in American universities of able young European scholars who are preparing to teach American courses in their own countries. Precedents for the exchange of experts and students have thus been set and further exchanges are proposed. Cultural relations such as these may offer a sounder basis for world understanding than do mechanical advances in transatlantic communication or transportation.

V

American Courses

AMERICAN courses are the report on American civilization which colleges and universities make to the nation and the world; out of that report American curriculums are constructed. These courses fall into three categories: first, introductions to American civilization for freshmen and sophomores, conducted either within one department or jointly by more than one; second, the body of the curriculum, made up of advanced undergraduate and graduate courses on American themes almost invariably conducted within separate departments; third, upperclass proseminars and graduate seminars in American civilization, always conducted in interdisciplinary terms and designed to integrate these departmental courses.

The first and the second category include familiar courses found in a majority of American colleges and universities. As such courses need no description, they are merely enumerated below with a brief note on their contribution to American Studies. But a few courses in these two categories and all those in the third are new; examples of these novel courses are described, both as exemplifications of the aims of American Studies and as suggestions for teachers and administrators who are looking for opportunities to expand their curriculums. Certain of the institutions which now offer such new courses are named. Highly specialized graduate seminars are usually omitted as irrelevant. Courses on the relations between America and foreign civilizations are not mentioned under the departments which offer them but are reserved for special examination as a unit.

AMERICAN COURSES

Back of the account of American courses which follows lie certain principles announced in the preceding chapters. First, the pattern of these courses is the complex design of American life and not the artificial sequence which specialism imposes on the offerings of an academic department. Here may be seen the fundamental diversity of human experience within which the student should eventually find an equally fundamental unity — a functional, not a departmental, unity. Second, many more courses than can be combined in one curriculum are described, to provide full data from which each college can select what is pertinent to its own situation but not to urge any institution to add this or that course. Third, the success with which individual colleges have drawn on their peculiar resources is illustrated by courses not generally appropriate because they can be given only by specially equipped men or institutions, and also by courses which are no longer offered because the men who initiated them have removed to other campuses. Fourth, instruction in American civilization ideally should be conducted to a considerable degree through independent study, but it is here tabulated almost exclusively as course work since education in the United States is conducted almost exclusively in those terms. For that unfortunate situation the author of this volume disclaims more than a small fraction of responsibility. (It should be emphasized that the listing of courses and citing of institutions where they are offered are merely suggestive and in no sense exhaustive.)

INTRODUCTORY COURSES IN AMERICAN CIVILIZATION

The initiation into American Studies for freshmen and sophomores is most often a departmental course in the general history of the United States, which needs no description. Several institutions announce a course entitled American Civilization, which is occasionally an introduction to American history under a new name. More inclusive are the surveys of American culture taught jointly by history and English (Simmons, Omaha), by history and political science

(Shorter), by history, English, and philosophy (Mills), or by a department of American institutions (Florida).

Three examples will illustrate what is done in these inter-disciplinary courses. One is a well-established unit in the well-established curriculum in general education in Columbia College: American Economic and Political Institutions. This follows a year's course in contemporary civilization; like that course it is taught by men from several departments. It first surveys and defines the features of the American tradition which differentiate it from European civilizations, then explores contemporary economic and political institutions with a view to clarifying current trends and current problems. Out of this course has come a widely respected anthology, *The Shaping of the American Tradition*, edited by Louis M. Hacker.

The course entitled Interpretation of American Institutions was first offered in the general education program at Harvard in 1947-48. General readings for the course include De Tocqueville, *Democracy in America*; Adams, *The Education of Henry Adams*; Bryce, *The American Commonwealth*; Myrdal, *An American Dilemma*; Turner, *The Significance of the Frontier in American History*; and Veblen, *The Instinct of Workmanship*. The methods of study employed by these authors, the scope of application of their observations, the knowledge presented, its relevance to contemporary institutions, and the quality of the works as sources of enjoyment are discussed. The course is taught by one instructor.

The American Heritage at Roosevelt College is designed specifically for undergraduates who propose to major in American Studies and deals with these topics: geographical backgrounds, the puritan mind, eighteenth-century religious liberalism, intellectual background of the American revolution, growth of the democratic ideal, development of educational ideals, the frontier, the industrial revolution, religious thought and institutionalization, social experiments and reform movements, impact of the Civil War, development of the fine arts and literary culture, rise of the American city, growth of the scientific spirit. The attention given to the humanities in this course at Roosevelt underscores the fact that these introductory surveys are usually limited to materials in the social sciences.

ADVANCED COURSES ON AMERICAN THEMES

American courses for upperclassmen and graduate students (both groups frequently must register in the same courses — not always to the advantage either of themselves or of their instructors) are almost always taught within one or another of the academic disciplines. A few advanced undergraduate courses (other than proseminars) are conducted outside those disciplines, however. At the College of St. Mary of the Springs courses in American civilization and American thought are taught in a separate department of American civilization, but it does not appear that the courses themselves are in any way unusual.

Stimulating are five unusual upperclass courses at Barnard College, open to American Studies majors and to other students. American Sources for Creative Writing is a study of the sources used by selected writers for fictional and nonfictional portrayal of American life; each student is given opportunity to acquire source material of her own and is assisted in using that material in creative writing. The Arts in American Civilization, while perhaps not exactly unique, is unusual in the way in which it traces the growth of two traditions of design in America, one derived from Western European sources and the other from the immediate experience of a people living under democratic institutions in a machine economy, and then studies the interaction of these two traditions in architecture, painting, literature, and music, cartoon strips, and the motion picture. Regionalism in the United States is a study of the characteristic cultures of various regions, with special attention to regional literature as it has been influenced by English, French, and Spanish culture.

53

The Legend of America deals with some of the basic literary and cultural traditions which have influenced world opinion of America, such traditions as the brave new world, the holy commonwealth, the noble savage, the Franklin legend of the natural man, the land of the free, the Yankee trader, the Lincoln legend of homespun wisdom, the self-made man, the melting pot, Titanism, movieland, the Roosevelt legend of the good neighbor. The Structure of Learning in America examines the fundamentals of learning, the spread of education, the varieties of training, the structure of colleges and universities, the foundations for research and higher learning, books and libraries, and the commercialization of knowledge, and compares our American system with the organization of the fields of learning in other countries.

Observers who are familiar with the foreign area programs conducted during the last war have said that, useful as they were in a military emergency, peacetime instruction in the American area is best conducted not through new courses (as is often necessary in studying a foreign society) but through existing departmental courses. Such is the general opinion also of people in American Studies, provided that this departmental instruction is drawn together by a conference or seminar. But these well-conceived courses at Barnard raise the question whether it might not be profitable to supplement departmental courses on American themes by more than interdisciplinary conferences and seminars.

The resources for American Studies in departmental courses may be summarized as follows:

Anthropology. The anthropologists perform three services for American Studies. They survey the general culture of the North American Indian and, in particular, his culture on the Plains, in the Southwest, and in the Pacific Northwest. They are turning their attention to contemporary civilization within a region, such as the Southeast (North Carolina). And they are beginning to study the American people as a whole, as witness the Population of the United States (Columbia) which examines our national and racial origins, our biological and geographic adjustments, our migrations, and our socio-political backgrounds. Anthropology and Contemporary Civilization (Stanford) shows what anthropology can contribute to the understanding of race relations, social work, international organization, and education. It is safe to predict that the anthropologists will in the future make even greater contributions to American Studies.

Geography. Significant courses deal with the geography of North America, now widely taught, and with the regional geography of the United States. The latter may take the form of a survey of all the regions (Stanford), of separate regions as New England (Harvard) or the South (North Carolina), or of urban areas (Pennsylvania). Useful also are courses in economic geography, also widely given, and on the conservation of natural resources (California, Iowa). The ignorance of geography among students suggests that Ohio State has done well to begin its American program in this field.

Economics. American economic history and the history and present problems of American labor clearly belong in an American curriculum. Other standard courses in economics also belong there if the instructor in any particular course conducts it in American terms as well as in the abstract terms of economic theory or of general business procedures. Students of American society can profit also from innovations not found in all institutions: Structure of American Economy (Columbia, Harvard), Farmer Movements (Wisconsin), and Economics of Technology (Antioch, Stanford). One such course surveys the influence of technological progress not only on economic but on political and cultural relations; a second examines the ways in which business practices (the patent system, for example) affect technological development.

Political Science. Two standard courses in political science always have a large place in an American program: American Political Thought and American Democracy. Two other courses are also useful when taught with some attention to their interdisciplinary implications: the American Constitution and American Political Parties. Unusual but relevant courses include a study of Congress, its problems and practices of membership, organization, and operation (Cornell) and of the constitutional, administrative, and political position of the president (Cornell). At least two disciplines are involved in Problems in American Federalism (Harvard) and in Government and the American Economy (University of Washington).

Although it is possible to use the same material in fresh and distinctive fashions in more than one department, students occasionally complain of repetition in an interdisciplinary program. One solution of this problem is to provide a jointly conducted course in an area common to more than one department. At Virginia, for example, there is only one introduction to American political thought and institutions, taught by the departments of political science, history, and economics and carrying credit in all three.

Sociology. The character of the standard courses in sociology is usually determined by the attitude of the instructors. If they present the family, urban and rural communities, population, housing, social disintegration, and reconstruction only through statistics, a student of American civilization can learn little from them; he can learn a great deal if they are presented as social relations.

The courses in four relatively new areas of instruction in sociology all relate to an American curriculum. First, American culture as a whole is being interpreted through its major institutions: economic organizations, religion, government, the family, education, social welfare, and recreation (Yale), or through social thought as developed by Sumner, Cooley, and others (Pennsylvania, Columbia, Yale). Second, regionalism in the United States is most often handled in one course which examines all the regions, contrasts regionalism

56

with sectionalism, and discusses local and national planning;
occasionally, however, one region is singled out for attention
(Denver, North Carolina, Harvard). One university (Harvard) parallels a course on Boston in literature with one on
Boston in the terms of sociology. Third, racial and national
minorities were first studied as a whole and still are, but
national groups and likewise racial groups are now sometimes given separate consideration (Reed, Chicago, Pennsylvania, Yale). On the Pacific Coast Mexicans and Orientals may receive special attention (Pomona); in the South,
Negroes (Virginia, Missouri). Fourth, social stratification —
or, in less professional language, class and caste in America
— is the theme of courses which examine the social positions
and ideologies of rural and urban areas, the status of social
groups, types of the elite, and relations between stratification and political movements (Smith, Harvard, Columbia,
Pennsylvania).

As in all departments, unique offerings in sociology reflect
the interests of active scholars in the field. Instances are
courses on the middle class in American culture, personal
income and expenditure as an approach to American culture, and the organization of power in American society
(Columbia).

History. Instruction which follows the basic course in the
general history of the United States falls into five groups,
three well established and two still fluid:

Period courses — the colonial period, the Revolution, Civil
War and Reconstruction, recent history (most useful for
American Studies wherever cultural factors receive more
attention than do military activities);

Regional courses — the frontier (ubiquitous monument to
Turner), the West (usually concerned with movements and
ideas), and the South (taught sometimes as military but
more often as social history; most significant for American
Studies when one of several regional courses as at Iowa and
Chicago);

57

Diplomatic history (usually factual; as such, not as significant for American Studies as the newer courses in foreign
relations).

A fourth group of studies, not yet formalized, deals with
the history of the concepts of economics, political science,
religion, education, and natural science. Local conditions
determine whether these courses are taught by men in these
departments or by historians. Economic history of the United
States is handled by economists wherever they have had a
substantial interest in the relationship between present and
past; elsewhere it is handled by historians. Intensive study
of the history of the constitution, of political parties, and of
political philosophy is usually reserved for political scientists
but in some instances (Columbia, Yale, Chicago) it is shared
by the historians. The history of religion in the United States
escapes sectarian bias where it is administered by the department of history (Columbia, Harvard). The history of
American education, commonly taught in a department or
college of education, may take on wider meaning if interpreted as social and intellectual history (Harvard). Legal
history has likewise become a province of historians in a
few universities, either in a general course (Pennsylvania)
or in one limited to the development of early American
legal institutions (City College of New York). A unique
course in the history of American medicine (Pennsylvania)
and one in science and technology in the United States
(Wisconsin) are of great significance to American Studies.

The last group, likewise still growing rapidly, includes
courses variously described as the social, social and economic, intellectual, or social and intellectual history of the
United States. As is natural in a new field, these courses
differ from campus to campus not only in title but in content. They are nevertheless highly relevant to American
Studies, for they all systematize American culture within the
framework of time. Certain universities make a helpful distinction between intellectual and social-economic history

(Harvard, Princeton, Wisconsin, Stanford), but such a distinction will not become general until teachers of intellectual history become generally available.

Other important courses introduced in recent years are the Immigrant in American History (Harvard), the Progressive Movement (Chicago), the Public Domain (Chicago), and Folklore (see page 61). Agrarian Ideas in American Politics (Yale) examines the ideas and policies advocated in America from Jefferson to the New Deal, with special attention to European origins and parallels, agriculture as a national interest, the economic and social aspects of recent agricultural policies, and domestic and international controls of agriculture. The History of American Democracy (Stanford, Mills) traces the beginnings, the development, and the contemporary manifestations of democracy and considers the place of leadership in social, political, and economic life (at Mills, in the terms of the contributions of thirty distinguished Americans). A foundation for projecting history into the future is laid in an undergraduate course, the Changing American Scene (Pomona), which traces the growth and the changing characteristics of American life, emphasizing the effect of change on a sense of nationality.

It will be observed that in history, as in other disciplines, there is considerable opportunity for free experiment within the department at the undergraduate level, whereas the traditions of graduate study tend to hold research courses within the formal patterns of departmental specialism.

Art, Architecture, and Music. Here existing resources are scantiest, and here the needs of general education and of American Studies have recently led several institutions to set up new courses. Surveys of American painting and of American architecture are not numerous and yet they are no novelty. Perhaps even more useful are the new omnibus courses on art in American civilization which survey architecture, painting, and the minor arts from colonial times to the present century in relation to cultural history (Columbia,

Yale, Princeton). Courses in American music employ the same nontechnical approach and deal not only with the history of folk, popular, and art music in the United States, but with the growth of musical organizations and the relation between composition and performance (Stanford, Pomona, Smith). In a few instances more advanced courses are offered such as American Painting (Yale), Contemporary American Music (Cornell), and Current American Architecture, with especial attention to Frank Lloyd Wright (Wisconsin). The motion picture is sometimes noticed (New York, Antioch, Stanford, Southern California), but it has not yet been critically evaluated as a factor in our civilization — an undertaking which might very profitably be conducted within the framework of American Studies.

Literature. Although the history of the teaching of American literature is brief as compared with the history of the classic disciplines, an introductory course is now offered in all except a few colleges. Advanced courses, however, are limited in number in all but a few universities, and even there it is not customary to offer more than one graduate seminar annually.

Courses in American literature tend to fall into these categories, each of which is exemplified in all parts of the country:

Chronological periods or movements — colonial literature, the romantic movement, realism, contemporary literature (courses which often deal with ideas relevant to American Studies);

Literary types in America — the novel, the short story, the drama, the essay (courses which introduce the interdisciplinary student to the techniques of literature);

The regions in literature — the Northeast, the South, the Midwest, the Far West (courses which clearly correlate with regionalism in painting, music, and the social sciences);

Studies in individual authors (which usually investigate technique and ideas and sometimes environment).

60

AMERICAN COURSES

Any department of English which wishes to increase its usefulness to American Studies can do so by adding courses in any of these four categories, but particularly useful is the extension of regional courses to include not only the area in which the institution itself is located (in most instances, the only region now examined) but other areas of the United States. At least one English department (New York State College for Teachers) covers the nation with a well-coordinated set of four courses, organized by a teacher with a wide acquaintance of American life. A suggestive seminar title is Boston as a Literary Center (Harvard), which might conceivably be paralleled from New York, Philadelphia, and Charleston to San Francisco.

More unusual and especially significant for American Studies are the courses in native folklore and folk literature which spring up wherever devoted teachers appear (Indiana, Cornell, Denver, Utah, West Virginia). These courses often bring together the disciplines of literature, history, sociology, and anthropology; American materials are sometimes set against a European background or against a generalized background of human culture. Courses in American humor (Chicago, Pennsylvania State, California in Los Angeles, Louisiana State) likewise cut across departmental lines, especially when they deal with folk elements in humor.

Equally pertinent are courses in American English (Texas, Wisconsin, Michigan, Western Reserve, Colgate, Columbia) which consider the historical changes in vocabulary and pronunciation differentiating American English from British English, the regional differences in American pronunciation and vocabulary, and standards of usage in the United States — all viewed as phenomena in the history of general culture.

Under a variety of titles, literary interpretations of American ideals and particularly of our democratic tradition are presented for majors and, more often, for nonmajors in English (Iowa, Wisconsin, New Mexico, Wyoming, Maryland, Colorado, Pennsylvania State, Indiana). Stimulated in a few instances by World War II, these courses fit neatly into the emerging pattern of general education and may be expected to remain in the curriculum in one form or another — not as political propaganda but as a vehicle for synthesis.

The history of the American theater and of public address in the United States as taught by departments of speech is a further resource in the general field of literature (Dartmouth, Wayne, Michigan, Oklahoma, Southern California).

Philosophy. A one-quarter or one-semester course in the history of American philosophy is offered by a number of institutions and is essential to any American program which makes adequate recognition of the humanities. The course usually gives particular attention to Edwards, Emerson, Peirce, James, and Dewey; usually it relates these men to the social and intellectual history of the United States.

Advanced courses in American philosophy are few. They may deal in detail with one or another of the philosophers already named (Stanford), with such contemporary movements as humanism (Wisconsin, Columbia), or with neglected American thinkers in relation to characteristic phenomena of American life (Yale). When conducted in interdisciplinary terms, courses in the philosophy of American education focus the resources of two fields on concrete problems and major issues in contemporary America.

The task of drawing on the past and the present to envision the shape of things to come calls for the combined talents of statisticians, anthropologists, historians, and social and natural scientists. In limited areas, such as trends in income and population, prediction is now attempted. But scholars in individual disciplines naturally hesitate to attempt any large-scale projection of American civilization into the future. One department of philosophy, however, has the courage to offer an undergraduate course entitled Schemes for a Better World (Barnard). Here are appraised utopias of the past, current plans for the postwar world, and possibilities for achieving the good life in the more distant future. Tentative as the results of such an undertaking must always be, here is an opportunity for collaboration among the disciplines — a present opportunity which the pressures of existence may transform into a necessity.

Field Studies. Field studies of European civilizations and of American geology, archeology, and botany have been for some time a reputable part of the college curriculum, as have been excursions to American slums and art galleries. On the other hand, extended field trips for the study of the geography, the institutions, and the arts of the United States have usually been restricted to the elementary and secondary schools and to students preparing to teach in these schools. Notably successful are the carefully organized field tours of the New Jersey State Teachers College at Montclair. These include lectures, readings, guided travel, and reports, and cover six areas: urban life, New Jersey and the lower Hudson Valley, the central eastern region, the lower South, New England and French Canada, the continental United States.

Liberal arts colleges experimented with similar field stud· ies before World War II made travel difficult (Wichita, Oregon), and certain colleges (Bennington, Sarah Lawrence, Antioch) now require field study or field work of all their students. A field course on colonial life in Jamestown, Yorktown, and Williamsburg was for a time conducted by the College of William and Mary with the aid of local historical associations. There is a place in American Studies for expertly directed field excursions, both regional and national.

American and Foreign Civilizations. This area of knowledge is so important to Americans and to American Studies that courses on our foreign relations in all their aspects should be examined with special care.

An excellent foundation for the study of our cultural relations is laid by several departments in their courses which deal with our colonial past and in the many courses which examine the present in general terms. In courses of the first type, influences and borrowings are always discussed but in the second type, where comparison and contrast between American and foreign cultures are always possible, they are not always made. In other words, each of the several civilizations touched on is often discussed in its own terms and the course disintegrates into fragments.

Advanced courses focused directly on American relations with the world are too few. Here or there a department of literature offers work (never more frequently than in alternate years) in Anglo-American literary relations (Louisiana State, Brown), British-American travel literature (South Dakota), Franco-American relations (Princeton), German-American literary relations (Princeton), Slavic backgrounds of American literature (Dartmouth), or non-English influences on American literature (Maryland). Only one university, it appears, provides all three courses which might well be offered very generally throughout the country: Anglo-American, Franco-American, and German-American literary relations (Wisconsin).

Departments of history contribute regularly and very substantially to international understanding through their courses on American foreign policy and foreign relations. Typical are courses which examine the expansive forces of American national life in relation to an evolving foreign policy, to the varied international interests of Americans, and to such policies as the Monroe Doctrine, the freedom of the seas, the Open Door, and isolation. Very useful also are courses in the history of our relations with Latin America (Pennsylvania, Arizona), with Canada (Columbia), and with the Pacific (Colorado, Pomona).

Equally important is the extensive study of our foreign relations conducted by the political scientists, chiefly in the present tense but often against a historical background. One well-planned course on American foreign policy is divided into three units. The first unit deals with the machinery through which foreign policy is formed and executed: the president, the State Department, Congress, political parties and pressure groups, and public opinion. The second unit is a topical and historical study of American foreign policy and interests abroad; non-entanglement, the Good Neighbor policy, reciprocal trade policy, the Monroe Doctrine, recognition. The third unit examines current problems in American foreign policy and relations: postwar organization, currency stabilization, trade policy, international airways. Specimen subjects of more advanced courses are our contemporary Far Eastern and Latin American policies (Cornell) and nationalism in international relations (Harvard).

Perhaps most profitable for American Studies are the very few courses which attempt an over-all survey of the relationships between American and European civilization (Stanford, Yale). Topics considered are European influences on the United States in the fields of religion, agriculture, science, politics, law, aesthetics, and scholarship; their means of transmission; their growth and modification in America in the light of the frontier hypothesis and other environmental philosophies; the recent export of American ideas and institutions to the Far East, Latin America, and Europe.

Nowhere are the unfortunate results of excessive specialism more evident than here. Instruction in the civilization of foreign nations, not yet entirely adequate, is nevertheless substantial; even more extensive is instruction in American civilization. But we and the world outside rarely meet in the same classroom; America is disastrously isolated from Europe and from Asia by the oceans of departmentalism. No additions to college and university curriculums can contribute more to world understanding and likewise to American Studies than courses which in themselves bridge the Atlantic and the Pacific.

UPPERCLASS PROSEMINARS AND GRADUATE SEMINARS
IN AMERICAN STUDIES

The desirability of bringing students in an American curriculum together either for preliminary training in the techniques of interdisciplinary study or for a final survey of the American scene is evident to everyone. As those who direct these programs gain experience, they usually conclude that such a provision is not only desirable but essential. Several proseminars and seminars are now in operation; others are in active preparation; others are proposed.

Proseminars for undergraduates are conducted by the department of history (City College of New York, Johns Hopkins), by English and history (Brooklyn, Cincinnati), or by these two with others (Bryn Mawr, Maryland, Pennsylvania, Vassar, Wells). The proseminar at Yale, originally designed for seniors, is now taken by juniors as preparation for their study of American life. This proseminar is conducted by an interdisciplinary-trained member of the department of English with the close cooperation of a historian of ideas and a sociologist, with occasional assistance from a psychologist and an anthropologist. Human nature is outlined in general terms applicable to any national civilization, with particular attention to the relations and interactions between the individual, the framework of society, and the cultural and geographical environment. American materials are then examined within the terms of this generalized outline.

Barnard provides initial guidance for both juniors and seniors. The junior proseminar includes discussions, forums, and field trips, supported by readings both on the American tradition and on contemporary problems. Seniors meet in a conference group with members of the departments of economics, English, government, history, philosophy, and sociology.

More often a proseminar is provided only for seniors. Longest established is that inaugurated at George Washington in 1936-37 by the professor of American literature. Here students interpret American civilization through ten factors: geography, immigration, government, political-social-economic history, religion, philosophy, education, literature, other forms of communication of ideas, the arts and crafts. At Maryland, the conference course for seniors approaches American culture first through its general bibliography and then through close analysis of eight to ten important books which present several fundamental patterns of thought and conduct. An example of effective cooperation between history and English is the senior course initiated at Williams in 1940-41, Changing Factors in American Life. Planned and conducted jointly by representatives of both departments, this proseminar brings the major disciplines to bear on these topics: American society as interpreted by Henry Adams, the shift from a rural society to an urban community, the shift from economic individualism to corporateness, the shift from supernaturalism to naturalism, the shift from absolute to psychological standards in ethics, American art as related to these changing factors, the shift from the conception of isolation to a world power, the shift from romantic glorification of the past to a scientific sense of history, the synthesis of these factors in twentieth-century life.

The senior conference at Princeton deals each year with a different topic, one which involves more than one discipline and leads to some conclusions concerning American civilization as a whole. Topics have been the impact of racial and national groups on American life (1942-43), the diffusion of evolutionary ideas in the United States (1944-45), socialism and American life (1946-47), and the role of the elite in American civilization (1947-48). Out of the first conference came a volume of essays, *Foreign Influences on American Life* (1944). A committee plans each conference; one man directs it; men from several departments contribute; the students participate actively and creatively.

Compared with these well-tried conferences for seniors, graduate seminars are still in the experimental stage. Subjects and treatment differ widely from university to university; at Western Reserve a series of weekly lectures on a wide range of American topics has been presented by members of several departments, while at Brown the seminar deals with culture during the colonial period and is conducted by a man with an interdisciplinary training in American civilization.

A well-conceived seminar at Pennsylvania, Forces and Ideas in American Life, organizes major topics in a historical sequence. The first semester is devoted to four influences on the development of American civilization before the twentieth century: (a) the frontier, the backtrail, the sections; (b) democracy: the rights of man; patrician, equalitarian, and social democracy; European appraisals and American responses; (c) orthodoxy, transcendentalism, science, pragmatism and skepticism; (d) the factory, the city, and the farm: the challenge of industry, utopian solutions, revolt and reform. In the second semester, a cross section of America during the twentieth century is presented: (a) American capitalism: the triumph of business, traits of capitalistic culture, America's economic crisis, challenges to American capitalism; (b) social democracy: the New Freedom and the New Deal, the demand for the old freedoms, the plea for racial equality; (c) the world impact of American power: the lure of empire, the isolationist tradition, American internationalism; (d) secularism versus the search for truth: the spread of materialism, attacks on materialism, experiments in faith.

The reader is now asked to return to page 51 and reread the author's general statement concerning American courses, which should now have increased significance.

One of the values of the interdisciplinary study of American civilization lies, as has already been suggested, in the unusual degree of responsibility placed on the student himself. It is therefore appropriate for any institution to expand its American offerings not only through formal instruction in courses but through directed reading. Let the student of American culture go often to the library to read and to

AMERICAN COURSES

think, not forgetting that, in Emerson's phrase, Cicero and Locke and Bacon were once only young men reading in libraries — as were also Emerson himself, James, Sumner, and Veblen.

VI

The Minnesota Program

THE Program in American Studies at the University of Minnesota is described in detail to indicate how the parts of an interdisciplinary program fit together, from a course on American life for freshmen and sophomores through the curriculum for the B.A., the M.A., and the Ph.D. degrees and on to public lectures, concerts, and a quarterly journal of American Studies. The Minnesota program is at the moment the most extensive in the country, but it is not presented here as ideal either for Minnesota (it is now and will continue to be under constant revision) or for any other institution (built to fit Minnesota, it would be equally appropriate nowhere else). No reader will endorse all the features of the Minnesota program nor, it is hoped, reject them all.

The Program was organized by a committee named by the dean of the liberal arts college, the dean of the graduate school, and their respective executive committees. The curriculum for the B.A. in American Studies is one of several curriculums made possible under provisions for a liberal arts major in the college. The curriculum for the M.A. and for the Ph.D. degree was authorized by the dean of the graduate school and his executive committee, following precedent set by other interdisciplinary curriculums. The curriculum for the B.A. and the M.A. was initiated in the fall of 1945, that for the Ph.D. in the spring of 1946.

The original Committee on American Studies included two representatives of history (one of them the dean of the graduate school) and one representative each of literature, political science, art, sociology, journalism, and philosophy. The chairman of the Program is chairman of this committee. The teaching staff hold appointments not in American Studies but in the regular academic departments, and all courses in the Program (except the introductory course on American life, the senior proseminar, and the graduate seminar) are regular courses of those departments. The number of faculty members who teach American courses naturally varies from time to time, but in 1947-48 the instruction was supplied by forty-five teachers from eleven departments: history seven, English seven, sociology six, journalism six, economics five, philosophy four, political science three, geography two, philosophy of education two, art two, anthropology one. (These figures are not an exact index to the emphasis placed by the Program on any one departmental discipline.)

The present prerequisite for an undergraduate major in American Studies is a year's work (normally taken during the freshman or the sophomore year) in American history or in American Life. The committee hopes to extend the provisions for advising underclassmen and thus make it practicable to require both these courses and one in modern European history.

The course, American Life, is one of three courses in the Humanities in the liberal arts college, the others being The European Heritage and Humanities in Modern Europe. The course is offered by an informal department of General Studies but is directed and taught by people active in the Program — at the moment by one teacher trained in history, a second in English, and a third in American civilization. Each instructor is responsible for his section or sections but each is assisted from time to time by sympathetic specialists from various departments. The course is interdisciplinary in approach and employs the resources of history, philosophy, the social sciences, and literature (all through the printed page), art and architecture (through Kodachrome slides and exhibits), music (through recordings and concerts), the dance, and the motion picture.

The central theme of American Life is the unity within diversity, the diversity within unity which characterize life in the United States. Under unfavorable circumstances its diversity sharpens into violence; where differences are reconciled the life of the nation is deepened and enriched. This theme is pursued through three groups of topics: nationalism, regionalism, internationalism; individualism, democracy, minorities in a democracy; labor, the pursuit of happiness, the good life.

The argument may be summarized as follows:

First, within these United States, an appreciation of one's region and an understanding of the other regions which form the nation are a basis for sane patriotism. In world society an appreciation of one's own nation and an understanding of other nations are a basis for world-citizenship.

Second, a healthy individualism is possible only among free men in a free state. Democracy as a way of life is the cooperation of these same free men. The treatment of minorities is an index to the degree to which individualism and democracy are reconciled in such a state.

Third, Americans, utilizing their regional and national resources and their heritage from the Old World, act freely and yet together in labor, the pursuit of happiness, and the search for the good life.

Some notion of the materials and methods in American Life may be had from a summary of the unit on regionalism:

Sectionalism in the colonies, in the young republic, and in the Civil War — the historical record

Sectionalism versus nationalism — documents

Sectionalism interpreted in literature

Regionalism in the twentieth century: geographic, economic, political, sociological

Regionalism in literature: the Northeast, the South, the Midwest, the Far West

The regions in folk music — recordings
Regionalism in domestic architecture — slides
The regions in painting — Kodachrome slides
The relations between sectionalism, regionalism, and na-
tionalism.

The curriculum for the B.A. degree puts into execution
the two principles accepted as basic to all American programs: American civilization must be studied both in the
past and in the present, and it can be understood only from
the interdisciplinary point of view. The program is based
also on two other principles not always accepted elsewhere.
First, it attempts to give equal emphasis to four areas of
American civilization, those represented by history, by literature, by philosophy and the fine arts, and by the social
sciences. (History is here separated from social science not
only because it is in itself a major area in American Studies,
but also because history becomes one of the humanities
whenever it is concerned more with values than with facts.)
This four-way division is still an experiment, open to modification. After it has been in operation for several years, the
committee will be in a position to determine whether such
a program is as effective as the more familiar curriculum
of a double major in history and literature supported by
courses in other disciplines.

Unusual but not unique is the second principle underlying
the Minnesota program — that within these four required
areas the individual student shall have all possible freedom
in the choice of courses. The practice sometimes followed
elsewhere, of requiring all students to take much the same
courses, has the obvious advantage of assuring them of a
common body of knowledge. But free election of courses
within the general scheme set by the committee has the
equally obvious advantage of allowing each student to work
out for himself a sequence of courses to fit his own concerns
and capacities. The aim, then, is maximum flexibility within
the framework of a four-dimensional curriculum.

The undergraduate concentration for a time totaled forty-eight credits (Minnesota operates on the quarter system), including six in a senior proseminar in American Studies and from nine to twelve in approved American courses in each of the four fields: (1) history, (2) literature, (3) philosophy and art, (4) the social sciences (anthropology, economics, geography, philosophy of education, journalism, political science, and sociology). Approved courses for the B.A. and for advanced degrees are listed below (page 76).

To provide undergraduates with data for comparing their own with another civilization, they were urged to devote part of their elective hours in the junior and senior year to courses in a foreign culture. As this recommendation was not always followed, it has now been made a requirement and the concentration for the B.A. has been expanded to include as a fifth field a foreign culture or a closely related group of cultures.

The integration of this interdepartmental curriculum is the personal responsibility of each student. As a senior he has the help of a professor trained in American civilization and of other seniors in the required proseminar in American Studies. The topics in this proseminar are adapted to the needs of each class and differ from year to year. During 1947-48 the students spent two quarters on classic commentaries on American life and the third quarter on the James family in relation to the American scene.

Candidates for the M.A. degree follow either of two plans offered by the graduate school. The majority elect Plan B, in which they present at least forty-five quarter-credits distributed among the four fields of history, literature, philosophy and fine arts, and social sciences. (As only one year is required for the master's degree, the committee on American Studies is not inclined to add the fifth field of foreign backgrounds to these requirements.) Under Plan B no thesis is required, but Plan A calls for a minimum of twenty-seven hours distributed among three of the four fields and a thesis on some aspect of American civilization in the terms of more than one discipline. Under both plans each candidate is given a written examination by a standing committee (interdepartmental) of the Program and an oral examination by his own committee (also interdepartmental). As teaching positions are still almost invariably departmental, candidates for the M.A. so organize their work that they have a competence in one department equivalent to a major for the B.A. They also meet the general requirements of the graduate school, including knowledge of a foreign language.

Candidates for the Ph.D. spend a minimum of three years (including relevant work done for the M.A. by holders of that degree) in graduate study of the history and the present status of civilization in the United States. Candidates must study in all five of the fields now required for the B.A., including a foreign culture or group of cultures. Candidates for the Ph.D. are given a written examination in each of these fields and a general oral examination. The dissertation deals with a topic which involves two or more departmental disciplines. Candidates who propose to teach so organize their programs that they have a competence in one department equivalent to that required for the M.A. They also meet the general requirements of the graduate school, including knowledge of two foreign languages.

The graduate seminar is conducted by one man trained within a department and a second trained in American Studies. The topics and the approach vary from year to year, but in 1947-48 the seminar attacked three problems. In the fall quarter the students were introduced to the bibliographical aids and the central themes in the five required fields, with particular attention to the period from 1620 to 1800. In the winter quarter, the agrarian tradition during the nineteenth century was explored in history, the social sciences, literature, and the arts. In the spring quarter, the impact of industrial capitalism on American civilization during the nineteenth and the twentieth century was examined.

AMERICAN STUDIES

Courses approved for 1948-49 (the list is revised annually) follow. These are standard courses offered regularly; special summer courses are listed elsewhere. (Certain courses are open to undergraduates, others to graduate students, and still others to both.)

History. The American Colonies, American History since 1900, The American West, Minnesota and the Northwest, American Diplomatic History, American Economic History, American Social and Intellectual History, Early American Social and Intellectual History, American Folklore, Immigrant in American Life, Seminar in American History.

Literature. American Literature, American Colonial Literature, American Novel, American Short Story, American Drama, Recent Literary Criticism, T. S. Eliot, The Midwest in Literature, The Far West in Literature, American Speech, American Naturalism, Seminar in American Romanticism I and II, Seminar in American Realism.

Philosophy and Fine Arts. American Philosophy, Philosophy of John Dewey, Design for America, Philosophy in Literature, Art in the Americas, Art and American Civilization, American Music.

The Social Sciences. The American Indian, Indians of the Plains, Indians of the Southwest, Geography of North America, Historic Geography of North America, Labor Problems and Trade Unions, The Cooperative Movement, Government Regulation of Business, Modern Philosophies of Education, The School and the Social Order, Intercultural Education, History of Journalism, Literary Aspects of American Journalism, Communication Agencies and Public Opinion, Interpretation of Contemporary Affairs, Principles of the American Constitution, American Political Parties, American Political Campaigns, American Political Thought, Problems of American Democracy, Government and the Economic Order, Social Organization, The Family, Social Life and Cultural Change, Theories of Social Reconstruction, Population Trends, Rural Community Organization, Rural Social Institutions, Topics in Urban Society.

America and Foreign Civilization (for the B.A. and Ph.D. degrees). Relevant courses, preferably concerned with one civilization or one cultural area, as approved by the candidate's adviser.

As courses in philosophy and the fine arts are few, students often find it impossible to enroll for more than the minimum number of credits in this group. What might appear to be an excessive number of approved courses in the social sciences is in reality no more than are desirable if each student is to have full opportunity to build his own program. As the Program in American Studies does not train departmental specialists, departmental seminars are ordinarily approved only in the two areas where students often have special competence, history and literature.

Initiated in 1946, the Summer Program in American Studies offers, through two sessions of six weeks each, a variety of courses for the B.A., the M.A., and the Ph.D. degrees. In addition to the general presentation of American civilization, special attention was given in 1947 to science and American civilization and in 1948 to America's cultural relations with Europe.

The fundamental instruction in American Studies is conducted by permanent members of the faculty, but each year the director of the summer session makes it possible to offer new courses by visiting professors who bring variety and stimulus to students and resident staff. During the three summer quarters from 1946 through 1948, the following new courses have been introduced by various departments and by the Program:

History. The Cultural Heritage of Colonial America, History of the South, Major Interpretations of American Civilization, History of American History.

Literature. Contemporary American Literature, The Negro in American Literature, The Southwest in Literature, Melville and the Modern World, Origins of Realism.

Philosophy and Fine Arts. Philosophical Crises in American Religious Thought, Regional Art in America.

Social Sciences. The American Character, The Constitution and Social Change, Conflicting Issues in American Education, The Press and the Public.

Science and American Civilization. History of Science in the United States, History of American Medicine, History of American Agriculture, Evolutionism in American Thought, Influence of Science on American Literature Prior to 1860.

America and Foreign Civilizations. Influence of Europe on American Culture, Anglo-American Cultural Relations to 1860, Influence of European Philosophy in American Thought.

Visiting professors who have taught summer courses on American subjects, either by departmental appointment or through special provision for American Studies made by the director of the summer session, include thirty-one guests from England, Canada, seventeen states, and the District of Columbia. Their departmental affiliations were as follows: history six, history of science two, history of agriculture one, political science five, journalism three, literature seven, philosophy three, music three, art one.

Students and members of the committee on American Studies have occasionally met for dinner and a talk on an American topic. These sessions have been so profitable that they will probably be continued regularly. For students and the public the Minnesota Program supplements classroom instruction with convocation addresses, concerts, showings of motion pictures, and afternoon lectures. Examples are a series of monthly lectures on the following subjects, "Classical Influences on American Culture," "England to America," "The Liberal-Democratic Compromise in France and America," "The Germans of Minnesota," "Scandinavian Influence on American Life," and "The Orient and America"; six programs tracing the growth of the American motion picture; a series of illustrated lectures on photography in the United States; five lectures on American music; a series of three recitals of American music; a series of three recitals of

American folk music. Lectures and recitals are presented weekly during the summer session and less frequently during the academic year.

Each summer a one-week, non-credit institute in American Studies is conducted, both for teachers and for the non-academic public, in cooperation with the Center for Continuation Study. The center provides lecture and lounge rooms, bedrooms for students from outside the city, and meals at a moderate fee; the Program provides the staff, made up of members of the summer faculty and additional guest speakers. The program for 1946 illustrates the general character of the three institutes which have thus far been conducted.

Monday, July 15

The Place of American Studies in Secondary and Higher Education, Tremaine McDowell

The Cultural Resources of North Star Country, Meridel LeSueur

American Studies: A Survey, Arthur Bestor

The American Novelist and American Society I, James T. Farrell

The Music of the American Negro, Sterling A. Brown

Tuesday, July 16

Classroom Techniques in American Studies: Literature and the Fine Arts I, Robert Carlson

Great Documents in the History of American Civilization, Mr. Bestor

American Philosophy Today, Herbert Schneider

The American Novelist and American Society II, Mr. Farrell

Immigrant Songs and Ballads, Dean Theodore Blegen

Wednesday, July 17

The Humanities in Modern Europe: Background for American Studies, Alburey Castell

Techniques in Social Studies I, Edgar B. Wesley

AMERICAN STUDIES

American Folkways, Philip D. Jordan

Social Obligations of the Novelist (public lecture), Mr. Farrell

Documentary Films for American Studies, Mr. McDowell

Thursday, July 18

Techniques in Literature and the Fine Arts II, Bertha Handlan

The Negro in American Culture (public lecture), Mr. Brown

High Culture and Popular Culture, Alfred Kazin

The American Novelist and American Society III, Mr. Farrell

American Folk Music (a program of recordings), Lyman Newlin

Friday, July 19

Techniques in Literature and the Fine Arts III, Miss Handlan and Mr. Carlson

Techniques in Social Studies II, Harmony Brugger

The American Novelist and American Society IV, Mr. Farrell

Canada and the United States: The Entangling Alliance, George V. Ferguson

Social Hour

Saturday, July 20

Techniques in Social Studies III, Mr. Wesley

Review of the Institute, Mr. McDowell

The character of the public reached by the institute may be seen in the following tabulation of the sixty-seven registrants for 1946: teachers from the public schools of fifteen cities and towns in Minnesota and of Spokane, Washington, staff members of the boards of education of four communities in Minnesota and of Cedar Rapids, Iowa, members of the faculty of seven colleges in Minnesota and of Adelphi College (New York), Hood College (Maryland), Denison University (Ohio), Central Washington College, and Oregon State College, members of the staff of three public libraries in Minnesota, a book reviewer, a radio editor, and members of the general public. The institute for 1947 emphasized two topics, folklore and science in America (the special theme for that year's Summer Program). The institute for 1948 likewise dealt with the current theme of the Summer Program, America's cultural relations with Europe.

The University radio station, KUOM, broadcasts American Studies lectures and recitals, convocation addresses, and similar activities through both the regular year and the summer session. The station also cooperated with the Program in a daily classroom broadcast of Sterling Brown's summer course, The Negro in American Literature, and of Denis W. Brogan's summer course, The American Character. Alburey Castell's course on American philosophy is broadcast during the year. KUOM originated a series of programs on American folklore under the direction of Philip Jordan and maintains a summer program of American folk music.

The Committee on American Studies with financial support from the University of Minnesota, cooperation from the University of Minnesota Press, and the assistance of scholars and of nonacademic authorities throughout the United States, proposes to publish a quarterly journal of American Studies. The journal will be addressed to all who are concerned with American civilization — both within and without the academic world, inside and outside the United States.

Such a program as that conducted at Minnesota can be initiated and maintained only with the encouragement and the active aid of the administration of a university, the dean of a liberal arts college and a graduate school, the director of a summer session, a radio station, a center for adult education, a press, and the staff of all the departments concerned. Although this particular program would be inappropriate in any other university, there are on almost every campus the materials and likewise the need for an American curriculum adapted to that institution.

VII

Region, Nation, World

AMERICAN civilization is studied most effectively by a college or university which is studying at the same time local institutions within the United States and foreign civilizations beyond our national boundaries. Likewise an American curriculum is most effective when it combines national materials with materials which are both more and less than national. One example of the latter approach is the reduction of American society to its component parts in the study of class and caste in the United States, and a second, in the study of the racial and national groups in America. More fully developed and most useful to our purpose is the division of the United States into its regions as charted by geography, economics, sociology, history, literature, painting, domestic architecture, and folk music. The study of national culture may therefore very properly be supported (and if necessary corrected) on the one hand by regionalism and on the other by internationalism. Thus American Studies move toward the reconciliation of the tenses, the reconciliation of the academic disciplines, and a third long-range goal, namely, a reconciliation of region, nation, and world.

Civilization in the United States and American Studies have thus far been discussed chiefly in relation to actual achievements in the past and the present. Any examination of our regional and our national culture in relation to world society must be conducted with some regard also to unachieved ideals and to the future. Three documents provide the basis for the comments on region, nation, and world which follow.

The first document, that on regionalism, was written by a professor of philosophy born in California, educated at the University of California and Johns Hopkins, and teaching at Harvard when in 1902 he read his essay on "Provincialism" as a Phi Beta Kappa address at the State University of Iowa. Josiah Royce defined *province* as any part of a national domain which is conscious of its own unity, takes satisfaction in its customs and ideals, and feels a sense of distinction from the rest of the nation. *Provincialism* he defined as the tendency to possess such ideals and customs, their totality in themselves, and the local patriotism which cherishes them. Royce thoroughly approved of what he called provincialism, as calculated to root Americans more deeply in their own locale and thus to strengthen resistance to conformity and to mass hysteria. His provincialism we today call regionalism.

In the mid-eighteenth century, the local loyalty of a British American was to his colony and his national loyalty to the Empire; in the late eighteenth century an American's local loyalty was to a commonwealth or a section, and his national allegiance was to the new republic. In the nineteenth century loyalty to a section, North or South, was intensified until Calhoun proclaimed the right of a minority to nullify national law; when nullification failed, his section seceded. In the North Hawthorne declared that New England was as large a lump of earth as his heart could encompass; when the South declared its independence, he accepted the dissolution of the Union as inevitable. But these two spoke for a minority; the Civil War proved that the military and political resources of national unity are more powerful than are those of sectionalism.

During the latter half of the nineteenth century, this sectional feeling nevertheless persisted and even increased wherever sharp economic competition developed. But there was also in each area (particularly in the older areas) an increased interest in the rest of the nation. In finance the result was the export of capital from the Northeast to the South and the new West, often to the advantage of debtor as well as creditor. In population the result was the export of manpower from the Northeast and the South. In literature it was the local color movement, the exploration of the unusual in customs and character in the South, North, and West. Even though self-interest was present in all these activities, they lacked the destructiveness of acute sectionalism and, where the pressure of competition was not too great, they contributed more to national unity than to disunity.

In the years since Royce addressed Phi Beta Kappa at Iowa, the Far West and the South have resisted exploitation with increasing vigor, and economic ill will has continued to spread among the sections. At the same time Royce's idea of "wholesome provincialism" has expanded into our idea of regionalism. Whereas sectionalism is based on the assumption that each area is or may become a unity within itself, the concept of regionalism is based on the belief that unity exists only in the nation of which the regions are subareas. Whereas the section exists in and for itself, the region exists for both itself and the nation.

Unlike nineteenth-century local color which was limited to the field of literature, regionalism today is an inclusive movement. Regionalism is botany and agriculture: the United States is divided into palmetto country, piñon country, desert country, and delta country, long grass and short grass country, winter wheat and spring wheat country, and many more. Regionalism is planning for river valleys: the United States is divided into the valley of the St. Lawrence, the Tennessee, the Missouri, the Columbia, the Colorado. Regionalism is city versus country. It is the nation divided into market areas, newspaper coverage areas, service areas for industry, federal reserve areas, time zones, and baseball leagues.

The most frequent common denominator in these regionalisms is geography, and it is geographically that regionalism in the related arts most often coincides with regionalism in economics, political science, and sociology. Regionalism in literature, painting, and music is the interpretation of human experience in the symbols which the artist finds in that area of the United States with which, either for life or for the moment, he is most familiar. This does not mean that regional art is merely local. It employs unmistakably regional language to express the universal — otherwise it is not art. But it may be folk art, especially in the field of American music.

If a region is not to relapse into a section, it must constantly share with other regions what it possesses. The vehicle for that sharing is most often the printed page — that is to say, books on the regions as interpreted by both popular and scholarly geographers, anthropologists, sociologists, political scientists, economists, and men of letters. Earlier in the century, New York publishers were sometimes too provincial to recognize that young regional artists were doing good work and it was necessary for local magazines and local presses to prove that Manhattan is not America. This having been proved, few New York houses are today content unless they publish a series on the rivers, the lakes, the mountains, the cities, the folkways, or the foods of the United States. The interests of all the regions will be best served, however, if local as well as national outlets continue to be available for regional expression.

The most influential centers of regionalism have been and will continue to be located at some distance from Megalopolis. One such is in the Carolinas. Here is an interest alike in the past and in the present — an interest furthered, of course, by local pride but guided by scholarship, particularly at the University of North Carolina and Duke. The movement has many ramifications, including the South Carolina Poetry Society, the North Carolina Folklore Society, the South Carolina and especially the North Carolina Historical Societies, and vigorous sociological organizations. Ready at hand are

outlets for regional writers: the Carolina historical quarter-
lies, the *South Atlantic Quarterly,* and nearby the *Virginia
Quarterly Review.* Most influential of all is the ably directed
University of North Carolina Press. Thus sociology, literature, history, and anthropology cooperate in the study and
the criticism of regional aspects of Negro as well as white
culture. At the same time these scholars and these journals
deal with national and world topics, for it would be grossly
unjust to describe their activities as exclusively regional. All
that is necessary is opportunity for regional expression —
never the domination of expression by regionalism.

To most Americans loyalty to a local community is tangi-
ble, but loyalty to a vast continental nation is an elusive
abstraction. A helpful bridge between the two is regional
patriotism, a particularly effective bridge in the United States
because our people are unified in national terms but diversified in regional terms. Our differences in speech, for example, are familiar to all of us and yet these differences are
less extreme within the United States than they are within
England — where they contribute to rather than contravene
nationality. American customs likewise show regional variants, but variants not as great as those, for example, in
France — where they are not destructive of French nationality. Out of regional loyalties, then, Americans can and frequently do build national patriotism. And in the same fashion students synthesize the knowledge which they gain from
regional courses into a fuller understanding of these United
States.

The second document, that on nationality, was written by
a second professor of philosophy, born in Vermont, educated
at the University of Vermont and Johns Hopkins, and teaching at Columbia (after experience at Michigan, Minnesota,
and Chicago) when in 1917 he published "The Principle of
Nationality" in the *Menorah Journal.* Confronted by the fact
that *nationalism,* once a reputable word, has fallen into dis-
repute because of the crimes committed in its name, John

Dewey chooses the term *cultural nationality* to describe the principle which he defends. Six factors are involved in nationalism and nationality. For the latter, two factors are necessary: some community of language and some unity of culture. For nationalism four factors are necessary: these two plus territory (the economic element) and a sovereign state (the political element). Neither nationalism nor nationality requires factors five and six but each is intensified by their presence: community of race and community of religion.

National loyalty is compounded of both cultural nationality and politico-economic nationalism, as has been tragically illustrated since Dewey wrote his essay. The Germans and the Japanese, for example, have prostituted their cultural nationality to promote the aims of inflamed nationalism. Profoundly moved by religion and by race, Irish Catholics, Jews, Hindus, and the Moslems of India seek to extend nationality into nationalism. Even though Dewey's distinction between the two is not universally accepted, it will be adopted here as necessary to a discussion of national loyalty.

The patriotism which came out of the American Revolution was and still is this same compound of cultural nationality and political nationalism. The latter became an accomplished fact when the federal constitution was adopted. In the young and still weak republic this nationalism was strengthened by the sense of achievement which followed our westward expansion against the opposition of a few Indian tribes, our victory over Great Britain in the War of 1812 when Britain was occupied by other foes, and our bold stand against continental European aggression in the Monroe Doctrine — a stand which our citizens mistakenly believed we maintained alone but which was actually underwritten by England. Thus protected by what was then our geographical isolation and by the self-interest of our mother country, we were left free to make ourselves eventually the great power we earlier, and fallaciously, assumed we were.

Cultural nationality, on the other hand, was for many years tentative and fragmentary in the United States. At the end of the Revolution political nationalists demanded the instant creation of an American culture: new manners, new language, new literature, new painting, new music. Of course such matters cannot be achieved, as can nationalism, by acts either of war or of legislation. There could be no nationality until the one-time Europeans who made up society in the United States learned to respond each in his own way to the stimuli of the New World.

Inevitably the progress of nationality was not only slow but uneven. Thus when the Hudson River School tried to paint America, their techniques were European and the results were pleasing but imitative; only in our century have American painters mastered the techniques which they have borrowed and devised. But on the other hand, Emerson, Thoreau, Hawthorne, Melville, and Whitman more than a century ago wrote each in his own fashion concerning the United States and the total result was a literature recognizably American. When the Civil War broke out, the Americans had reached a considerable degree (but by no means a totality) of cultural maturity. In other words, they were no longer dominated by what they took from other civilizations; they digested these borrowings and made them part of themselves. When this takes place, a people has achieved cultural nationality.

American nationalism and nationality have sometimes been in conflict and sometimes in agreement. When our politico-economic nationalism led us into war with Mexico a hundred years ago, cultural nationality protested through the voices of statesmen and men of letters. During the period of the Civil War nationality accepted the divergencies between regional culture in the South, the Northeast, and the West but nationalism could not accept the secession of a section. There was an attempt to invoke cultural nationality as a sanction for the Spanish-American War, but the net results for the United States were clearly nationalistic. If, as many of us believe, both world wars were necessary to the defense of our culture and our national sovereignty, our participation in both was dictated alike by nationality and by nationalism.

The events of American history indicate that nationality becomes dangerous when it is the tool of diseased nationalism, and that the latter becomes diseased when economic or political pressures are too powerful. Symptoms of disease in American nationalism have been excessive concern with the acquisition of land, an inclination to make the state all-powerful, national egocentricity in relation to our own regions or to the world as a whole, and self-glorification either through romantic inflation of the past or braggart glorification of the present. In its final state unhealthy nationalism takes the form of isolationism. The best corrective to these abnormalities is the subordination of economic and political activities to cultural nationality.

The contrast between sectionalism and regionalism is generally comparable to the contrast between isolationism and cultural nationality. American sectionalists and American isolationists are self-centered and inward looking; they seek self-aggrandizement without regard for other groups or peoples. On the other hand, American exponents of regionalism and of cultural nationality recognize the values and rights of other regions and other nations; they extend the principle of self-determination from self to others.

At a moment in history when the need for world cooperation has never been more evident, it may seem ill advised to argue for any variety of national patriotism. And anyone associated with American Studies will be suspected of chauvinism if he argues for national loyalty in the United States. But we have reared a generation of young Americans to be so suspicious of the word *propaganda* that they often reject unimpeachable wisdom if they believe that someone has something to gain from its acceptance. Now a second generation is growing up to be equally suspicious of the term *national loyalty.* One of the functions of American Studies is, therefore, to guide students in American courses to a repudiation of political and economic nationalism and to an acceptance of cultural nationality.

The third document was written by a business executive born in Indiana, educated in the liberal arts college and the law school of the University of Indiana, successful as president of Commonwealth and Southern, but defeated as Republican candidate for president of the United States. *One World,* written in 1943 when Rommel was still in North Africa and the Japanese were in China, seems almost as far removed from us today as Royce's essay of 1902. Naïve yet honest in its idealism five years ago, *One World* is today a moving document in the history of utopianism.

After traveling around the world in forty-nine days, Wendell Willkie concluded that American thinking must hereafter be world wide and that American principles must hereafter be translated into action. More specifically he urged that in the Near East we should no longer maneuver for the control of local resources by playing off native forces against each other, that we should learn to work with Russia, that we should protect our reservoir of good will all over the world by following ideals rather than expediency.

Students of our relations with Europe know that the United States has never been as isolated from the rest of the world as our lusty nationalists would have us believe. Before the Revolution Englishmen in New England laid foundations for American individualism in the Puritan doctrine of private judgment and for American democracy in the doctrine of the compact. Frenchmen and Englishmen contributed the materials for the Declaration of Independence. Through the nineteenth century, ideas and events in the United States were less often results of thought and action in Europe than parallel developments from similar stimuli. Thus the Jacksonians, when they attempted to revise the frontier doctrine of the self-sufficiency of the common man to fit the new conditions of the factory system, were facing the same industrial revolution with which their contemporaries wrestled abroad. Likewise when the United States and Europe reached '48, the romantic rebellion in politics, religion, literature, and the arts had reshaped culture on both sides of the Atlantic. Both our rejections and our acceptances of the ideas of Darwin and of Marx, somewhat delayed in transit, helped bind us to the Old World. During the present century the currents of influence have gradually reversed their direction until today they flow more often from West to East than from East to West. Regardless of their direction, they tie us to Europe.

In a manner not paralleled elsewhere the cultural nationality of the American people synthesizes the many cultures of Europe. In 1800 our citizens were overwhelmingly of English descent. Not only was their native speech English but their culture was English. Today only a minority of us are descended from English forebears; more than half of us are non-English in our origins. In other words, every group among us is now a minority group and every college course on minorities in the United States is concerned with every American citizen. We are a nation of nationalities unified by the new American culture. But while that culture was taking shape, the world has shrunk beyond our comprehension. The countries from which our ancestors voyaged by sail and by steam have moved westward across the Atlantic. Today England rises in the fog just off the coast of Maine; France lies not far beyond the tip of Long Island; Spain replaces Cuba off the Florida shore; behind them all looms Russia. And these nations into whose daily activities we shall soon be peering through the windows of television are the same nations from which came our ancestral cultures. These strangers on our doorstep are not strangers; regardless of the languages which they speak, they are our grandparents and our cousins – some of them still our friends, others of them estranged from us, but all our blood relations and contributors to that fresh and new yet not always fortunate synthesis of civilizations which is American civilization. The study of American culture is, then, a microcosmic examination of European culture as well as a macrocosmic examination of regional society.

It is significant also that as soon as our own republic was founded, its citizens began to dream articulately of one world. Here, as often in American history, the Christian tradition was influential and we envisioned a peaceful universe in which brethren dwell together in amity under God. Such for example was the eventual goal of Benjamin Rush when he proposed a secretary of peace for the American cabinet. Gathering strength through the nineteenth century, the movement reached its high point under the stimulus of Elihu Burritt just before North and South took up arms. Equally well-meant campaigns for peace followed but they failed, often because they were based not as much on the brotherhood of man as on nationalistic or even isolationist concepts — like, for example, the Ford peace ship. Americans have dreamed also of a secular world state ever since Timothy Dwight envisioned a league of nations in the eighteenth century. But whenever a Woodrow Wilson makes concrete proposals for a league of nations, nationalism reacts even more violently than it does against the abstractions of an Elihu Burritt. In general, however, the temper of our idealism, the form of our government, and perhaps our ignorance of the difficulties of international cooperation bred by our geographical detachment, encourage us to dream more often and more rosily of a republic of man than do the citizens of any other nation.

Again it is possible to set up a rough equation of attitudes in the United States. As regionalism is to cultural nationality, so cultural nationality is to world cooperation. That is to say, loyalty to one's region may expand into loyalty to the nation, and the latter may in turn expand into the brotherhood of man. And as sectionalism is to national isolationism, so national isolationism is to world imperialism (one world is equivalent to one empire). This last sin America has only feebly attempted by force of arms, but our economic imperialism did not escape Willkie in the Near East nor does it escape a student of American civilization today. But, without minimizing the dangers incipient in that imperialism, most Americans conclude that it is at the moment a less potent deterrent to the creation of a world community than is our isolationism.

Continuing with this assessment of our strengths and our weaknesses, any student of American culture will admit that our sectionalism may have been and perhaps still is stronger than our regionalism, and likewise that our politico-economic nationalism may still be stronger than cultural nationality. But we all know also that the American ideal is a family of regions united in one nation and a family of nations united on the planet. Despite all unhappy discrepancies between aspiration and accomplishment, America's achieved realities and partly achieved ideals for region, nation, and world offer as sound a precedent for a community of man as has yet emerged anywhere in the world. At two points, then, American Studies can contribute largely to the creation of world order: first, through exploration and exposition of this unique American pattern of region, nation, world and, second, through the education of America for critical self-knowledge. Since a federation of the world can be formed neither out of zeros nor out of intransigent sovereign states, an enlightened American nationality is one of the essentials to an effective league of mankind. Self-knowledge is therefore a prerequisite to citizenship both in the United States and in a world community.

If students of American civilization participate in the building of this new world, it should be with full realization that the task will be completed neither this afternoon nor tomorrow morning. Certain obstacles at home have already been identified. The most powerful obstruction abroad is, according to Willkie, imperialism. He was heartened by the knowledge that men on the top level in England and elsewhere were searching for a formula which would remake the British empire into a true commonwealth, but he was alarmed by the fact that British foreign administrators have trained themselves for and have put all their capacities into the maintenance of the old order. Having thus paid everything they possess for a share in an empire, they are willing to admit that it is not a perfect empire, but they are not inclined to do themselves out of a job and go on the dole for life by admitting that world society has experienced or should experience any major change. They have their counterparts, of course, in all countries and in all professions.

Americans who bring to bear on the future a knowledge of the past and of the present realize how disastrous it is for hopeful parents, hopeful teachers, and hopeful clergymen to send young citizens out into life expecting that within five years or at the most ten they can remake the nation and the world to fit their own admirable ideals. Hope deferred maketh the heart sick and disillusioned young liberals make bitter fascists. Here, as the historian recognizes, we move toward a distant and not an immediate goal. Here Willkie revealed his naïveté and here *One World* is utopian. Lacking historical perspective, living chiefly in the present, and trained in the methods of technology and big business, Willkie assumed that a congress of the world could be convened in the not-too-distant future. But the historian knows that electing a truly representative parliament of man is a long-range, long-time project. He knows also that we shall never achieve that goal unless we push toward it as eagerly as we pursue an objective which can and must be reached in six months. What should keep us sprinting at top speed in this race — which is actually no hundred-yard dash but a marathon — is the crash of the atomic bombs which from time to time we drop at our own heels.

REGION, NATION, WORLD

Wendell Willkie has in Walt Whitman an ally wiser than himself, an ally who saw the same vision but covenanted with the future, not the present, for its fulfillment. The vision seen by both men Whitman recorded in symbols drawn from our regional and our national experience, but transmuted by his mystical faith into the language of all mankind. Thus Whitman and Willkie and all who share their dream are laying a foundation for the reintegration of man in the coming age of the modern.

Years of the modern! years of the unperform'd!
Your horizon rises, I see it parting away for more
    august dramas,
I see not America only, not only Liberty's nation
    but other nations preparing,
I see tremendous entrances and exits, new combina-
    tions, the solidarity of races,
I see that force advancing with irresistible power on
    the world's stage . . .
I see men marching and countermarching by swift
    millions,
I see the frontiers and boundaries of the old aris-
    tocracies broken,
I see the landmarks of European kings removed,
I see this day the People beginning their landmarks
    (all others give way);
Never were such sharp questions ask'd as this day,
Never was average man, his soul, more energetic,
    more like a God, . . .
His daring foot is on land and sea everywhere, he
    colonezes the Pacific, the archipelagoes,
With the steamship, the electric telegraph, the
    newspaper, the wholesale engines of war,
With these and the world-spreading factories he in-
    terlinks all geography, all lands;
What whispers are these O lands, running ahead of
    you, passing under the seas?

95

AMERICAN STUDIES

Are all nations communing? is there going to be but
  one heart to the globe? . . .
The perform'd America and Europe grow dim, re-
  tiring in shadow behind me,
The unperform'd, more gigantic than ever, advance,
  advance upon me.